Joyce Appleby on *Thomas Jefferson*
Louis Auchincloss on *Theodore Roosevelt*
Jean H. Baker on *James Buchanan*
H. W. Brands on *Woodrow Wilson*
Alan Brinkley on *John F. Kennedy*
Douglas Brinkley on *Gerald R. Ford*
Josiah Bunting III on *Ulysses S. Grant*
James MacGregor Burns and Susan Dunn on *George Washington*
Charles W. Calhoun on *Benjamin Harrison*
Gail Collins on *William Henry Harrison*
Robert Dallek on *Harry S. Truman*
John W. Dean on *Warren G. Harding*
John Patrick Diggins on *John Adams*
Elizabeth Drew on *Richard M. Nixon*
John S. D. Eisenhower on *Zachary Taylor*
Paul Finkelman on *Millard Fillmore*
Annette Gordon-Reed on *Andrew Johnson*
Henry F. Graff on *Grover Cleveland*
David Greenberg on *Calvin Coolidge*
Gary Hart on *James Monroe*
Hendrik Hertzberg on *Jimmy Carter*
Michael F. Holt on *Franklin Pierce*
Roy Jenkins on *Franklin Delano Roosevelt*
Zachary Karabell on *Chester Alan Arthur*
Lewis H. Lapham on *William Howard Taft*
William E. Leuchtenburg on *Herbert Hoover*
Gary May on *John Tyler*
George S. McGovern on *Abraham Lincoln*
Timothy Naftali on *George H. W. Bush*
Charles Peters on *Lyndon B. Johnson*
Kevin Phillips on *William McKinley*
Robert V. Remini on *John Quincy Adams*
Ira Rutkow on *James A. Garfield*
John Seigenthaler on *James K. Polk*
Hans L. Trefousse on *Rutherford B. Hayes*
Tom Wicker on *Dwight D. Eisenhower*
Ted Widmer on *Martin Van Buren*
Sean Wilentz on *Andrew Jackson*
Garry Wills on *James Madison*

ALSO BY TIMOTHY NAFTALI

Khrushchev's Cold War:
The Inside Story of an American Adversary
(with Aleksandr Fursenko)

Blind Spot:
The Secret History of American Counterterrorism

U.S. Intelligence and the Nazis
(with Richard Breitman,
Norman J. W. Goda, and Robert Wolfe)

The Presidential Recordings:
John F. Kennedy:
The Great Crises, Volume 1 (July 30–August 1962)
(Editor)
The Great Crises, Volume 2 (September–October 21, 1962)
(Coeditor with Philip Zelikow)

One Hell of a Gamble:
Khrushchev, Castro, and Kennedy, 1958–1964
(with Aleksandr Fursenko)

George H.W. Bush

Timothy Naftali

George H.W. Bush

THE AMERICAN PRESIDENTS

ARTHUR M. SCHLESINGER, JR., AND SEAN WILENTZ,

GENERAL EDITORS

Times Books

HENRY HOLT AND COMPANY, NEW YORK

Times Books
Henry Holt and Company, LLC
Publishers since 1866
175 Fifth Avenue
New York, New York 10010
www.henryholt.com

Henry Holt® is a registered trademark of
Henry Holt and Company, LLC.

Distributed in Canada by H. B. Fenn and Company Ltd.
Frontispiece: Portrait of President George H. W. Bush © CORBIS

Library of Congress Cataloging-in-Publication Data
Naftali, Timothy J.
  George H. W. Bush / Timothy Naftali. — 1st ed.
    p. cm.—(The American presidents series)
  Includes bibliographical references and index.
  ISBN-13: 978-0-8050-6966-2
  ISBN-10: 0-8050-6966-6
  1. Bush, George, 1924– 2. Presidents—United States—Biography.
3. United States—Politics and government—1989–1993. I. Title.
  E882.N34 2007
  973.928092—dc22
  [B]   2007026217

Henry Holt books are available for special promotions and
premiums. For details contact: Director, Special Markets.

First Edition 2007

Printed in the United States of America

1 3 5 7 9 10 8 6 4 2

For my mother, Marjorie Naftali,
and in memory of Frederick Holborn
and Arthur M. Schlesinger, Jr.:
three beloved students of human nature

Contents

Editor's Note

The president is the central player in the American political order. That would seem to contradict the intentions of the Founding Fathers. Remembering the horrid example of the British monarchy, they invented a separation of powers in order, as Justice Brandeis later put it, "to preclude the exercise of arbitrary power." Accordingly, they divided the government into three allegedly equal and co-ordinate branches—the executive, the legislative, and the judiciary.

But a system based on the tripartite separation of powers has an inherent tendency toward inertia and stalemate. One of the three branches must take the initiative if the system is to move. The executive branch alone is structurally capable of taking that initiative. The Founders must have sensed this when they accepted Alexander Hamilton's proposition in the Seventieth Federalist that "energy in the executive is a leading character in the definition of good government." They thus envisaged a strong president—but within an equally strong system of constitutional accountability. (The term *imperial presidency* arose in the 1970s to describe the situation when the balance between power and accountability is upset in favor of the executive.)

The American system of self-government thus comes to focus in the presidency—"the vital place of action in the system," as Woodrow Wilson put it. Henry Adams, himself the great-grandson and grandson of presidents as well as the most brilliant of American historians, said that the American president "resembles the commander of a ship at sea. He must have a helm to grasp, a course to steer, a port to seek." The men in the White House (thus far only men, alas) in steering their chosen courses have shaped our destiny as a nation.

Biography offers an easy education in American history, rendering the past more human, more vivid, more intimate, more accessible, more connected to ourselves. Biography reminds us that presidents are not supermen. They are human beings too, worrying about decisions, attending to wives and children, juggling balls in the air, and putting on their pants one leg at a time. Indeed, as Emerson contended, "There is properly no history; only biography."

Presidents serve us as inspirations, and they also serve us as warnings. They provide bad examples as well as good. The nation, the Supreme Court has said, has "no right to expect that it will always have wise and humane rulers, sincerely attached to the principles of the Constitution. Wicked men, ambitious of power, with hatred of liberty and contempt of law, may fill the place once occupied by Washington and Lincoln."

The men in the White House express the ideals and the values, the frailties and the flaws, of the voters who send them there. It is altogether natural that we should want to know more about the virtues and the vices of the fellows we have elected to govern us. As we know more about them, we will know more about ourselves. The French political philosopher Joseph de Maistre said, "Every nation has the government it deserves."

At the start of the twenty-first century, forty-two men have made it to the Oval Office. (George W. Bush is counted our forty-third president, because Grover Cleveland, who served nonconsecutive terms, is counted twice.) Of the parade of presidents, a dozen or so lead the polls periodically conducted by historians and political scientists. What makes a great president?

Great presidents possess, or are possessed by, a vision of an ideal America. Their passion, as they grasp the helm, is to set the ship of state on the right course toward the port they seek. Great presidents also have a deep psychic connection with the needs, anxieties, dreams of people. "I do not believe," said Wilson, "that any man can lead who does not act . . . under the impulse of a profound sympathy with those whom he leads—a sympathy which is insight—an insight which is of the heart rather than of the intellect."

"All of our great presidents," said Franklin D. Roosevelt, "were leaders of thought at a time when certain ideas in the life of the nation had to be clarified." So Washington incarnated the idea of federal union, Jefferson and Jackson the idea of democracy, Lincoln union and freedom, Cleveland rugged honesty. Theodore Roosevelt and Wilson, said FDR, were both "moral leaders, each in his own way and his own time, who used the presidency as a pulpit."

To succeed, presidents not only must have a port to seek but they must convince Congress and the electorate that it is a port worth seeking. Politics in a democracy is ultimately an educational process, an adventure in persuasion and consent. Every president stands in Theodore Roosevelt's bully pulpit.

The greatest presidents in the scholars' rankings, Washington, Lincoln, and Franklin Roosevelt, were leaders who confronted and overcame the republic's greatest crises. Crisis widens presidential opportunities for bold and imaginative action. But it does not guarantee presidential greatness. The crisis of secession did not spur Buchanan or the crisis of depression spur Hoover to creative leadership. Their inadequacies in the face of crisis allowed Lincoln and the second Roosevelt to show the difference individuals make to history. Still, even in the absence of first-order crisis, forceful and persuasive presidents—Jefferson, Jackson, James K. Polk, Theodore Roosevelt, Harry Truman, John F. Kennedy, Ronald Reagan, George W. Bush—are able to impose their own priorities on the country.

The diverse drama of the presidency offers a fascinating set of tales. Biographies of American presidents constitute a chronicle of wisdom and folly, nobility and pettiness, courage and cunning, forthrightness and deceit, quarrel and consensus. The turmoil perennially swirling around the White House illuminates the heart of the American democracy.

It is the aim of the American Presidents series to present the grand panorama of our chief executives in volumes compact enough for the busy reader, lucid enough for the student, authoritative enough for the scholar. Each volume offers a distillation of character and career. I hope that these lives will give readers some understanding of the pitfalls and potentialities of the presidency and also of the responsibilities of citizenship. Truman's famous sign—"The buck stops here"—tells only half the story. Citizens cannot escape the ultimate responsibility. It is in the voting booth, not on the presidential desk, that the buck finally stops.

—Arthur M. Schlesinger, Jr.

George H.W. Bush

Introduction

Two American presidents—Gerald Ford and Bill Clinton—had different names (Leslie Lynch King Jr. and William Jefferson Blythe III) before they introduced themselves to the American people, but George Bush is the first who came to be known by a different name after he left the White House.

What's in a name? In the story of George Herbert Walker Bush, it means a lot. Over the course of his life he has had an unusual number of names, shedding each one as if it were an outer skin. As a boy he was known as "Poppy," symbolic of being a favorite grandson, but a name he came to detest by the time he reached early adulthood. Then, for a short while, he was "Pop." Following World War II, when he wanted to seem older and needed to strike out on his own, he became George H. W. Bush, oil entrepreneur and family man. Entering politics in the early 1960s, he dropped the initials to become the more populist George Bush. Thirty years later, after leaving public office and dedicating the George Bush Presidential Library and Museum, Bush embraced the initials again to differentiate himself from his son George W. Bush. The elder Bush wanted to get out of the younger Bush's way. The "H. W." returned, and he exited stage left.

"Who is George Bush?" was a taunt associated with his most stubborn political critics, but it was also asked by many throughout his public life. Like his name, Bush's political persona was protean and mystified many observers. Self-described, at various times, as a Goldwater conservative, a "responsible conservative," and a Reaganite, Bush nonetheless supported many of Lyndon Johnson's Great Society programs, had a moderate voting record as a congressman and a philosophically mixed record as president. As a result, even after decades on the national scene, George Bush's public image never quite seemed in focus. This would be a severe handicap for him as president. When the economy soured in 1991, his poll numbers swiftly collapsed because Americans lacked any strong personal commitment to him. Yet what weakened Bush's bid for a second term would provide an unexpected boon in his retirement. When George W. Bush's administration got tangled up in a seemingly endless war in Iraq, the public rediscovered George H. W. Bush and many began to wonder whether they had ever understood or fully appreciated the Bush who had refused to march on Baghdad.

This book will attempt to bring George Bush's presidency into focus. Even had George W. Bush not been elected, his father's presidency would have deserved a good hard look. More by accident than by design, it straddled four pivotal years in international politics. The Cold War ended, and a new international system, still dimly understood nearly two decades later, emerged. Although less epochal, important changes were also occurring at home. After Ronald Reagan had shown in 1980 that campaigning for the center was no longer the secret to electoral success, American politics began a descent into bitter polarization. With all of these historically significant things happening around him, was Bush merely a bystander, like Zelig in Woody Allen's film of the same name, or did he matter, in a larger sense?

For four or eight years, an American citizen is asked to be at once chief of state, head of government, and commander in chief. Already in the early nineteenth century, Thomas Jefferson called the presidency a "splendid misery," and by the twenty-first century it has become a job that is nearly impossible to do well. We still use presidents as a shorthand to chart our history and continue to categorize these individuals as "great," "near great," and so on. But can one accurately categorize an entire presidency? Presidents are human beings, who make mistakes and occasionally great decisions. Does Jefferson's embargo suggest limits to the greatness of the president who approved the Louisiana Purchase? Can the opening to China significantly repair the severe damage to Richard Nixon's reputation from Watergate? How does one weigh the internment of Japanese Americans in assessing Franklin Roosevelt's four terms?

For a period of two years, from 1989 until early 1991, George H. W. Bush made a series of very good decisions, some of which deserve to be considered great. Among modern presidents, his handling of the end of the Cold War belongs in the same category as Franklin Roosevelt's decision to emphasize the war with Hitler over the war against Japan after Pearl Harbor, Dwight Eisenhower's studied restraint in the face of Soviet provocation and domestic anxiety at the end of the 1950s, and John F. Kennedy's management of the Cuban missile crisis.

This book offers a portrait of a very human leader. Driven by almost insatiable ambition and competitiveness—seen at its worst in his handling of the Iran-Contra scandal and in the tactics used occasionally on his behalf in political campaigns—Bush would nonetheless serve and govern with humility. Although Bush was emotional and a worrier, his key decisions as president were wise and considered. And while lacking in rhetorical gifts or charisma, he led an administration that impressed adversaries and reassured allies in a period of rapid and dramatic international change. His presidency may not be remembered as great but, as we shall see, George Bush successfully answered the call for greatness when his country required it. And without his brief moment in power, neither of the iconic presidents before or after him—Ronald Reagan or Bill Clinton—would have enjoyed the same measure of success.

1

Poppy

On June 12, 1924, a second son was born to Prescott and Dorothy Walker Bush of Milton, Massachusetts. Named after his fabulously wealthy and entrepreneurial maternal grandfather, George Herbert Walker (the namesake of golf's Walker Cup), little George Herbert Walker Bush was soon called "Poppy" to distinguish him from his grandfather, who was "Pop" to his extended family. Less than two years later, Prescott Bush took an executive position with U.S. Rubber in New York City, and the young family moved to Greenwich, Connecticut. Prescott was on a corporate fast track, helped in part by friendships he had formed and family connections. His first job came as the result of an offer from a fellow member of Skull and Bones, Yale College's oldest and most legendary secret society. Not long after reaching New York City, Prescott left U.S. Rubber to begin a long and distinguished career with the international investment house W. A. Harriman and Company, owned by the family of his Yale classmate Roland "Bunny" Harriman and managed by his father-in-law, Bert Walker.

The Bushes were High Church Episcopalians. They went to church regularly, but they considered a person's relationship to God, as indeed one's own emotions, to be a private matter. Pres and Dottie were strict and formal and expected the same from their children. Self-discipline, however, was not synonymous with lacking a sense of fun. Their home was full of music; Pres loved to sing. And from the moment he could walk Poppy Bush was encouraged to play games and to have a passion for competition. Both of his parents were good athletes and always played to win. Pres and Dottie enjoyed tennis together and Pres, like his father-in-law, was an accomplished golfer, and in 1926 he became chairman of the United States Golf Association's Championship Committee.

In the family, which ultimately grew to four boys and one girl— Prescott Jr., George, William, Jonathan, and Nancy—the children were taught early on to take responsibility for themselves. It was up to each one to decide where he or she would go to prep school. Since his adored older brother, Prescott Jr., had chosen Phillips Academy in Andover, Massachusetts, George followed in 1937. He excelled at baseball and soccer and became the captain of both teams. He was also a leader off the field, eventually becoming the president of his senior class and a member of the editorial board of the student newspaper, the *Phillipian,* and—a mark of one of his interests to come—chairman of the annual charity drive on campus. As a senior he nearly died from a staph infection in his right arm. Surviving this ordeal, which required a lengthy stay in the hospital, may have given him a sense of mission, if not destiny.

Even as a young man, Poppy had a strong sense of self, and more than any of his siblings he internalized the family's culture of competition. (When Prescott Bush was a Republican senator from Connecticut in the 1950s, he became notorious for never allowing President Dwight Eisenhower to win at golf.) Yet as success brought yet more success for Poppy, his mother would remind him not to be self-centered, whenever possible not to use the pronoun *I,* and to avoid, at all costs, patrician pretension, which she colorfully termed the *La-Dee-Dahs.* Years later, when Bush was president, his aides would explain his peculiar speaking style as the effect of a lifetime of motherly admonitions not to claim credit for himself alone.

To an even greater extent George Bush drew upon his father, whom he idolized, for life lessons. Most significantly, George embraced Prescott's strong sense of service. Prescott Bush had signed up for the Yale battalion in the U.S. Army in 1917 and saw action with the American Expeditionary Force in France in 1918. After the Japanese bombed Pearl Harbor in December 1941, his senior year at Andover, Poppy hungered to follow in his father's footsteps and enlist as soon as he could in the great war of his generation. Even an admonition from Secretary of War Henry Stimson, Andover's graduation speaker in 1942, who advised the young men to stay in school, did not deter George from joining the military as soon as he turned eighteen in June. Nor did similar advice from his father. George Bush chose to become a naval aviator, earning his wings in June 1943 and becoming the youngest pilot in the entire U.S. Navy.

On a Christmas break his last year at Andover, Bush had met Barbara Pierce at a country club dance. Pierce, who was home from a girls' school in Charleston, South Carolina, was the daughter of Marvin and Pauline Pierce. Marvin was a director of McCall's Publishing Company, which produced mass-market women's magazines. After a brief courtship, Barbara would become the "girl back home" that George Bush would write to from his bunk and after whom he would name his airplane, for good luck. Before he left for the Pacific in 1943, he asked her to marry him

The U.S. Navy trained Bush in photographic intelligence, and it also matured him. "Coming out of a privileged background," Bush wrote forty years later, "I had had little exposure to the real world—to people from very different backgrounds. I went into the service as a gung ho kid, scared at times, becoming a Naval Aviator." He would fly a torpedo bomber that was also equipped with cameras. In early 1944 Bush reached Pearl Harbor onboard the *San Jacinto*, a converted light carrier. His first bombing run came in May against the Japanese positions on Wake Island. These bombing runs were extremely dangerous, and before long Bush would lose two of his close friends in action.

With the capture of Guam in August 1944, the U.S. military turned to the island barriers of Japan. Bush's squadron was given the responsibility for knocking out the radio transmission center on Chichi Jima, to blind Japanese intelligence to the steady forward movement of U.S. forces. On September 2, Bush flew his Avenger with its four 500-pound bombs into Japanese antiaircraft fire as he had done by now dozens of times. This time, however, some flak hit his plane. "There was a jolt," Bush later recalled, "as if a massive fist had crunched into the belly of the plane." Despite a cockpit that was filling with smoke, Bush steadied his throttle and continued aiming for the target. Dropping his bomb load, Bush then headed out to sea. He radioed to his two crewmen, John Delaney and Ted White, to get out of the plane and use their parachutes. Without hearing anything in response from the other side of the armor plate at the back of the cockpit, Bush unstrapped himself and climbed onto the wing. Failing to make a clean jump, Bush hit his head on the back of the plane and ripped his chute. Tumbling 2,000 feet into the water—moving faster because of the hole in his chute—Bush nevertheless escaped major injury. He deployed a small life raft and began paddling. A pilot seeing him in distress strafed Japanese ships on their way to capture Bush. A few hours later a U.S. submarine fished the young lieutenant out of the water. Bush was the only man of his plane to survive. Overcome by the experience and the loss of his crew, Bush cried in his raft as he awaited rescue. "I'm afraid I was pretty much of a sissy about it," he apologized to his parents in a letter sent the next day. He blamed himself for the deaths of Delaney and White. "I did tell them and when I bailed out I felt that they must have gone, and yet now I feel so terribly responsible for their fate, Oh so much right now."

Although he could have gone stateside after being shot down, Bush returned to his ship and flew another eight missions over the

Japanese-occupied Philippines. In November he went home with 58 missions and 126 carrier landings to his credit. On January 6, 1945, he married Barbara and was stationed in Virginia until he was mustered out after Japan surrendered in August. Only twenty-one years old, Bush was now a married man, with a distinguished flying cross, two gold stars, and the ghosts of the friends he had lost in war.

After experiencing combat, "going to Yale was like going to Kennebunkport in the summer," one of Bush's brothers later told biographers, referring to the family's vacation compound in Maine. Bush joined the swollen class of 1949 as a freshman in the fall of 1945. The fourth generation of the Bush family to attend Yale, George made a conscious effort to emulate his father's collegiate achievements and succeeded for largely the same reasons. His winning personality, good looks, and leadership qualities naturally drew people. Like Prescott, he was chosen captain of the Yale varsity baseball team more for the qualities he displayed in the clubhouse than for any prowess that he had on the field. Pro scouts who briefly cast an eye on the lanky, six-foot-two-inch, left-handed first baseman concluded he was a strong fielder who couldn't hit. George followed his father in doing work for the United Negro College Fund, and when he was inevitably tapped for Skull and Bones, his father's secret society, George lived up to the Bush family's progressivism in civil rights by being out-front in promoting the breaking of the society's color barrier.

George Bush's Yale experience was not exactly the carbon copy of his father's. Like most of the veterans flooding into college in 1945, he was older than the traditional freshman and was soon providing for a family. Although he joined a fraternity, the focus of his social life was the cramped apartment on Hillhouse Avenue in New Haven, where he lived with Barbara and their first child, George Walker Bush, who was born on July 6, 1946. There the Bushes did not always get favorable attention. Barbara would hang their son's diapers on a clothesline outside their apartment, and the Yale president, who lived a few doors down, would notice and others would complain.

After Yale, from which he graduated in three years, Bush remained true to family tradition by not following in his father's footsteps. Bush sons were expected to prove themselves to their fathers by making it on their own. Prescott Bush had refused to take a cent from his father, S. P. Bush, a sign of their troubled relationship, but it was also a source of virtue in his own mind. When his father died, Prescott passed his entire inheritance on to his sisters. As George Bush later admitted to a reporter, even after proving himself in World War II, he believed he had to get out from under the "shadow" of his father. George chose not to join W. A. Harriman in New York, which would have ensured him an excellent lifestyle, and he refused to take any seed money from his father. Instead he moved to Odessa, Texas, and took a job with Dresser Industries, an oil-field supply company owned by a family friend, Neil Mallon. Bush had some of the risk-taking panache of his grandfather Bert Walker in him, but he was also pleased to have the security of working for a man he knew. George and Barbara Bush found that they liked West Texas and the challenge that the oil business provided. In 1950 George raised $350,000 to go into business for himself with John Overbey, an independent oil operator in Midland, Texas. His father contributed $50,000, but most came from his uncle George Herbert Walker Jr. and from various family friends, including Eugene Meyer, the publisher of the *Washington Post*. He and his partner formed the Bush-Overbey Oil Development Company to trade in drilling rights. In 1953 the partners joined with William and Hugh Liedtke, two brothers from Tulsa, Oklahoma, to create Zapata Petroleum, named after the Marlon Brando movie *Viva Zapata!*, to begin drilling for oil.

Tragedy struck after the Bushes moved to Midland, Texas, in 1950. Their daughter, Robin, age three, contracted incurable leukemia.

Her death in 1953 hit the couple very hard. As so often happens when a couple loses a child, the marriage suffered. Barbara fell into a depression and George became more distant. As George tried to mask his own pain, Barbara focused more attention on their two remaining children, seven-year-old George W. and eight-month-old John Ellis Bush, nicknamed Jeb. Little George received the brunt of it. "She kind of smothered me," he would later say of his mother. By the end of the 1950s three more children were to join the family, Neil, Marvin, and Dorothy.

• • •

Prescott Bush was a trendsetter in yet another way for his son, by introducing the entire Bush family to politics. In 1950 he ran as a Republican for the U.S. Senate from Connecticut but lost in a very close election to William Benton. What had made the difference was some negative campaigning that implied that Bush was in favor of legalized abortion, not a popular stand in Connecticut, a heavily Catholic state. Two years later Prescott beat Abe Ribicoff in a special election following the death of Connecticut's senior senator, Brien McMahon. Prescott campaigned as an economic conservative but refused to identify with the right wing of his party. At an event with the famously anti-Communist senator Joseph McCarthy, he told the audience that though he shared the Wisconsin senator's concerns about communism, he did not like his methods.

In the Senate, Prescott Bush became one of the first Republicans to denounce McCarthy in that body. "Either you must follow Senator McCarthy blindly, not daring to express any doubts or disagreements about any of his actions, or, in his eyes, you must be a communist, a communist sympathizer, or a fool who has been duped by the communist line." Bush suffered no political damage from his courageous stand. Indeed, he became a favorite with the elite of his party. He was a solid Eisenhower Republican—pragmatic, pro-business, but also pro–civil rights and socially liberal. He played some golf with the new vice president, Richard Nixon, and the two men developed some respect for each other. Senator Bush, however, did not much like Nixon. "He's not much fun," he confessed to his family.

Prescott Bush had explained that a man should seek political office only after securing his family's finances. An amicable split among the Zapata partners in the late 1950s earned George Bush (with the help of his uncle) his first million. The Liedtkes took over Zapata's drilling operations on land, and Bush acquired full ownership of Zapata's offshore oil rig operations. (The Liedtkes would later transform their company, through a merger, into Pennzoil.) Now well off, though not wealthy by Texas standards, George moved his family to Houston, where he, too, turned his attention to politics.

Although he had attended Yale at a time when fellow students Brent Bozell and William F. Buckley Jr. were launching a new conservative movement, Bush had stayed out of political discussions as a young man. "Labels are for cans," he had told Barbara, who believed her husband's political views were much like Prescott's, social liberalism mixed with economic conservatism and marked by a preference, above all, for moderation. In 1963 the leaders of Houston's small Republican Party enlisted Bush to run for the party's county chairmanship. They wanted him to fend off a challenge from the far-right John Birch Society, which was becoming a political force in the South, spreading paranoid fantasies of international conspiracies of bankers and Masons who were driving the world toward collectivism. Birchers, as they called themselves, alleged that Dwight Eisenhower and most members of the Council on Foreign Relations were communist and that the United Nations was the first step toward an insidious world government. What helped them in the South, however, was their rigid opposition to civil rights legislation, which Birchers claimed was the product of communist influence.

Bush won the chairmanship of the Harris County Republican Party and then surprised some of his backers by seeking some accommodation with the Birchers as a way to expand the party's memberships. "He didn't understand," recalled Roy Goodearle, a local Republican fund-raiser, who had recruited Bush to run as county chairman and then found his approach to the Birchers naive. Bush, however, was laying the groundwork to run for the U.S. Senate in 1964 and believed he needed to unite all Texas conservatives to have a chance. What in retrospect seems an audacious leap by a neophyte made more sense in the dynamic political environment gripping Texas in the early 1960s. After Lyndon Johnson became vice president in 1961, the Democratic Party fell into a vicious internal struggle between conservatives and liberals. This split allowed a conservative Republican professor named John Tower to win the special election to fill Johnson's U.S. Senate seat. Suddenly Texas, long a bastion of the Democratic "Solid South," seemed to have a two-party system. In 1960 Houston was the largest metropolitan area in the nation to have voted for Nixon and appeared to hold promise as the core of a Republican Texas.

In the 1964 race for Texas's other Senate seat, Bush presented himself as a young and attractive right-winger in contrast to the sixty-one-year-old liberal Democratic incumbent, Ralph Yarborough. Espousing what he called "responsible conservatism," Bush campaigned against federal civil rights legislation at a time when African Americans were still the victims of systematic and structural discrimination. The civil rights bill introduced by John F. Kennedy and passed under Johnson was designed to provide federal muscle to wipe away segregation in public accommodations. As a longtime supporter of the United Negro College Fund, Bush presumably knew the hardships that black students faced, but he made a purely political calculation to take advantage of the fact that Yarborough was vulnerable in Texas because he had supported the bill. "The civil rights issue," Bush wrote to a friend, "can bring

Yarborough to sure defeat." Bush said he supported civil rights but explained that he was philosophically uncomfortable with the bill because it gave the federal government too much power. Meanwhile Bush also espoused foreign policy views that put him on the extreme of his own party, next to the Republicans' controversial presidential nominee, Senator Barry Goldwater. He opposed the first U.S.-Soviet arms control agreement, the widely popular partial test ban treaty negotiated in 1963 and ratified by a vote of 80–19 in the Senate.

Initially the strategy seemed to work. Bush stopped being a long shot and instead garnered national attention as the most likely Republican to pick up a Senate seat in the South. The syndicated columnists Rowland Evans and Robert Novak described him as "running as an orthodox conservative, a slightly refined Goldwater Republican." Most of the press commented more on his style than his substance. "He is dashing, handsome, articulate—and a tireless, colorful campaigner," wrote a reporter for the *Los Angeles Times*. "And to hear some Texas women talk about him, looks will be a factor in this race." Even the master strategist Lyndon Johnson worried that this upstart might defeat Senator Yarborough. As Yarborough lost his lead and the race tightened at the end, Johnson issued a statement and traveled to Texas to campaign for the Democrat.

Bush lost but ran ahead of Goldwater, who was swamped by Johnson throughout Texas and the United States. In winning 1.1 million votes, Bush outpolled any other Republican in Texas history and staked a claim on the future of the party in the South. But he took the loss hard. Bush never entered a race that he didn't expect to win. And there had been another cost. Bush knew that he had sacrificed some personal integrity in choosing to run as he did, and he seems to have felt some disapproval from Greenwich. His parents did not make the effort to come to Texas during the campaign, and some of his Republican friends in the East were overtly uncomfortable with how easily he had transformed himself into a

Goldwater Republican. Bush had turned his back on the moderate Republicanism of his father, who had retired from the U.S. Senate in 1962. And his campaign—at least his positions—had courted segregationists and Birchers. Even during the campaign, Bush revealed that he recognized there was a moral cost to what he was doing. "We must be sure we don't inflame the passions of unthinking men to garner a vote," he wrote to one of his more moderate supporters. "What shall I do?"

Bush's experience in 1964 did not temper his ambition, but it did bring some introspection. Spoiled by the attention, and probably flattered by his favorable reviews from national Republicans, Bush believed he had a real future in elective politics and was eager to try again. At the same time, Bush recognized that it had been a mistake to identify so closely with the Goldwaterites. He liked Goldwater, whom he found less extreme in person, but the rural voters that Goldwater brought to the polls were not Bush's people. Next time he would have to create his own coalition to win. Days after the election, Bush approached the Texas party chairman and suggested a way to rid the party of those he called "nuts." Bush apologized to his supporters and later to his pastor for seeming to tolerate racists and Birchers. "I'm ashamed," he admitted in a speech in the summer of 1965, for not having taken issue with the "irresponsibility" of Goldwater's most extreme supporters. To his pastor he said, "You know, John, I took some of the far right positions to get elected. I hope I never do it again. I regret it." At a public session at the University of Texas in June, he also recanted his opposition to Johnson's Great Society program. Yet this change of heart also had a touch of the expedient and the tactical. In an article in *National Review*, Bush argued, "We should re-package our philosophy, emphasize the positive, eliminate the negative, warn of the dangers of the left but do so without always questioning the patriotism of those who hold liberal views." Political observers at the time were saying that both his future and that of the Texas Republican Party lay in winning urban and suburban voters, including minorities and labor. And Bush made a more public effort among African Americans, supporting a black girls' softball team.

Setting his sights a little lower, in 1966 he ran for and won the congressional seat representing Houston, garnering 57 percent of the vote. His campaign manager was a close friend and tennis doubles partner, James A. Baker III. Baker, who was younger than Bush, nevertheless often acted as the older brother in what became a complex relationship, filled with what seemed like sibling rivalry as well as deep devotion. Baker was a superb political strategist. In this campaign Bush had run to the left of his Democratic opponent, the conservative Frank Briscoe. Bush's political tacking also drew positive reviews from national Republicans who were still licking their wounds after the Goldwater debacle. The growing support for Richard Nixon, viewed as a moderate as compared with Goldwater, was part of this process of self-definition occurring within the party, which benefited a fresh face like George Bush.

Just as important, this time George Bush's parents flew down to be with him on election day, and Prescott Bush showed his pleasure by working hard to increase the clout of the freshman congressman. The former senator began calling his old friends on Capitol Hill to see whether they couldn't secure a major committee assignment for George. Father and son set their sights on Ways and Means, the most powerful committee in the House by virtue of the role it played in shaping the federal government's budget and taxation policy. Its coveted positions rarely went to freshmen. Thanks to Prescott's connections—House minority leader Gerald Ford and former vice president Richard Nixon each put in a good word with Democratic committee chairman Wilbur Mills—George Bush got the job.

Bush's thinking evolved once he reached Washington; he had few, if any, settled policy ideas. What he had were tendencies: Bush

disliked extremism of any kind; he preferred to seek solutions outside of the federal government; he believed in a strong defense and
in strong support for the U.S. military; he preferred spending cuts
over higher taxes; and he opposed segregation and racial discrimination, but he was uncomfortable in having Washington mandate
good behavior.

Despite this conservative temperament, Bush proved to be pragmatic and emotional. He began to vote more like his father than
like Barry Goldwater. Quickly dropping any pretense to being a
Texas conservative, he allied himself with moderate, civic Republicans, who believed in the goals of the Great Society and the war in
Vietnam but wanted both to be managed more efficiently. Bush
showed his governing philosophy in how he responded to Lyndon
Johnson's calls for a surtax on individuals and corporations to pay
for Vietnam and the Great Society. With inflation rising and the fiscal 1968 budget expected to be $30 billion in deficit, LBJ was
looking for a 10 percent tax on the highest incomes. As a freshman
congressman in the minority party, Bush could have easily scored
political points by opposing the tax and pressing for cuts in Great
Society programs instead, especially since even the Democratic
chairman of the Ways and Means Committee, Wilbur Mills, opposed the surtax. But Bush revealed that his instincts were to find
common ground, to put himself in Johnson's shoes, to reach across
the aisle to Democrats and try to make government work. Bush
also showed a capacity for making tough political decisions. He signaled to the White House that he believed the president should tell
the American people that they could not continue to have "guns
and butter" forever and that some sacrifice was required. And then
to make his point, he offered to support cuts that would affect one
of Houston's major employers. In September 1967 Bush privately
told Secretary of the Treasury Henry Fowler that he saw the need
for the tax increase and believed he could vote for it "despite the

heavy mail from his District against it," and could also vote for a cut in NASA (National Aerospace and Space Administration) appropriations, "if there is Presidential leadership."

Although not a naturally philosophical man, Bush was comfortable with Edmund Burke's notion that an elected representative owed his constituents his judgment and was not simply a conveyor belt for their concerns, prejudices, and local interests. For the sake of the public good, Bush was prepared to sacrifice the interests of the many aerospace workers in his Houston district and to take the heat from conservative tax cutters.

He also took the risk of annoying some social conservatives. As a congressman, he embraced what had been his father's crusade for family planning. At a time when the use of contraceptives was illegal in Connecticut, Prescott and Dorothy Bush had been leaders in what later became known as Planned Parenthood. In 1965, in the case *Griswold v. Connecticut*, the Supreme Court had struck down the Connecticut law. George Bush became one of the sponsors of a bill ending the ban on mailing or transporting condoms. He also was the main sponsor of a bill that decriminalized the use of contraceptives. Indeed, he was so active in this cause that Wilbur Mills dubbed him "Rubbers," the current slang for condoms. Finally, Bush pushed for changes in the Social Security Act that provided federal assistance for family planning services.

But George Bush took his greatest political risk in shifting his approach toward issues of race and civil rights. He joined with a group of young moderate Republicans, including Bill Steiger of Wisconsin, William O. Cowger of Kentucky, and Charles E. Goodell of New York, who were concerned about urban issues. In the summer of 1967, with riots already having occurred in Cleveland, Newark, and Detroit, they sent a joint letter to President Johnson suggesting the creation of a Neighborhood Action Crusade to "defuse" tensions in the inner cities. Using as their model the air warden program in World War II London, the men suggested the formation of "quasi-volunteer organizations to work constructively in rallying the stabilizing influence that exists in the neighborhoods." "The overwhelming majority of Negro Americans," they wrote, "are dedicated citizens, strongly opposed to disorder and violence. Involvement of these, our fellow citizens, in keeping the peace within their own neighborhoods is essential to the resolution of the current crises in our cities." The commanding general of Johnson's War on Poverty, Sargent Shriver, responded favorably to the suggestion, adding, however, that this activity was already being performed by Community Action Agency officials in the cities.

The next year Bush fully upended his platform of 1964 by voting for the Civil Rights Act of 1968, whose centerpiece was a guarantee of open housing. He faced a storm of disapproval from many in his district and tried to soften the reaction by appealing to the critics' patriotism. Reminding them that he had taken a congressional trip to Vietnam, Bush asked why the black men fighting for their country could not expect the same rights to find a home for their families as the white men fighting next to them.

Bush's shifts were not simply a reflection of principle. Not wanting to rely on the racists and Birchers, Bush understood that he would need African American votes to defeat conservative Democratic challengers. He was also positioning himself to play a larger national role. A rising star in the Republican Party, he was asked to give one of the responses to Lyndon Johnson's State of the Union address in January 1968. That year he also set out to help Richard Nixon retake the presidency for the GOP. He reported to the Nixon campaign on the progress of organizing in Texas by Governor Ronald Reagan of California, one of Nixon's chief rivals. Senator John Tower believed that the best way to forestall a Reagan victory in the Texas primary was to run "a favorite son" campaign himself. Bush was not sure that this was wise, but he told Nixon's deputy campaign chief, Peter Flanigan, that "until the delegates are chosen he thinks it would be a mistake for him to break the united front of the Party's pro-Tower stance." Bush, who knew that he would run unopposed in the 1968 congressional election, also offered his friend and former partner Bill Liedtke of Pennzoil to the Nixon campaign as finance chairman in Texas.

The campaign that Bush was organizing was not a local one. In April 1968 his father's friends such as George Champion of Chase Manhattan Bank, Neil Mallon of Dresser Industries, and Albert Cole, the chairman of Reader's Digest, began writing Nixon to suggest that he consider the freshman congressman as his running mate. So, too, did Bush's friends. "As your finance chairman in Texas," wrote Bill Liedtke, "I am committed, and will back you up in whatever you decide. However, as I was reading your speech 'Toward an Expanded Democracy' wherein you mention what you want your Vice President to do and define your hopes for the independent sector under a decentralized government, I was struck with the fact that you were almost describing our congressman, George Bush." Nixon ultimately chose a moderate from the South, but it was Maryland governor Spiro Agnew, who would ultimately prove to be more conservative than Nixon had expected.

This unsuccessful campaign for the vice presidency only whetted Bush's political appetite. By the end of 1968, he had set his sights on running for the Senate a second time. Prescott Bush did not think the timing was right—which made the quest even more compelling for the young man on the make. Bush assumed he could beat Ralph Yarborough in a rematch. Believing that Lyndon Johnson's intervention had saved Yarborough from defeat the first time, Bush went out of his way to court the retiring president. On Inauguration Day 1969, instead of sitting with other happy Republicans to watch Richard Nixon's victory parade, Bush headed out to Andrews Air Force Base to wave good-bye to the Johnsons as they left for Texas. By all accounts, he was the only Republican in the crowd—certainly the only Texas Republican. Johnson may have shaken Bush's hand, but he did not notice the young congressman that day. However, when he was told about the gesture a month later, the former president invited George and Barbara Bush to the Johnson ranch.

The Bushes visited the Johnsons in the early spring so that Bush could sound out the former president on whether he would support Yarborough. Bush tactfully couched his inquiry in terms of whether Johnson thought it would be wise for Bush to risk his House seat to try for the Senate. "Son," Johnson replied, "the difference between being a member of the Senate and a member of the House is the difference between chicken salad and chicken shit. Do I make my point?" Bush then mishandled the encouragement, such as it was. At a press conference a little later, he seemed to imply that Johnson would be supporting him by saying that he had met the former president and discussed the Senate race, but Johnson "didn't say anything about him [Yarborough] nor did he say anything about favoring either me or Senator Yarborough." Tail between his legs, Bush later sent a transcript to the Johnson ranch to show that he had been misunderstood. Johnson, however, made clear that he would support the Democratic nominee, whoever it was.

At the same time, Bush also courted Richard Nixon's support. In the summer of 1969 Nixon invited Bush to his home in San Clemente, California, to discuss supporting his bid for the Senate. Although confident Bush would win, Nixon nonetheless promised a "soft landing" if he did not.

As in 1964, Bush's worst instincts emerged when he was in a competitive race. In his first race for the Senate he had compromised his political principles; in the second race he allowed his campaign to cut corners to raise the amount of money he felt he needed. Through his old friend Bill Liedtke, Bush received $106,000 from a special fund that Nixon's cronies had established to help Republicans in the South. Called the Townhouse Fund, after the building where it was managed in Washington's Dupont Circle neighborhood, it involved violations of the campaign finance laws of the time. Although no evidence ever came to light implicating Bush in any explicit decision to violate campaign laws, his decision to take money from this fund would later cause him problems as evidence of even darker secrets of the Nixon administration were revealed.

The 1970 campaign proved another disappointment. Bush's luck turned when Lloyd Bentsen, a man of Bush's generation and, also, of his political cast, defeated the liberal Yarborough in the Democratic primary. If anything, Bentsen was more conservative than Bush. Not only did Bentsen start with an advantage because most Texans were registered Democrats, but he enjoyed the firm support of the popular former governor John B. Connally. Bush, who had hoped for conservative Democrats to defect to him in a race against a liberal, had no chance against Bentsen. The 1970 race also highlighted the incoherence of Bush's political image. The first term of the Nixon administration saw in some respects a continuation of the Great Society. Although Nixon himself appeared to be equivocal about these measures, his lieutenants pushed for the creation of the Environmental Protection Agency and the passage of the Clean Air Act, which mandated automobile fuel efficiency standards for the first time. The Nixon administration also supported the creation of the Occupational Safety and Health Administration, which in 1971 would start mandating new standards in the workplace; the Philadelphia Plan, an affirmative action program that required construction unions working on federally funded projects to meet "goals" for the hiring of minorities; and the Family Assistance Plan, which mandated a guaranteed income for the poor and federalized state welfare programs. Bush loyally supported these policies in the election—having been one of the few southerners to vote for the Philadelphia Plan and the FAP—while once again professing to be a conservative. He also sponsored legislation calling for the creation of a national center for population and family planning under the Department of Health, Education and Welfare.

Although Bush needed no encouragement to run, he had appreciated Nixon's promise of a "soft landing" if he did not win. Even before the results were in, there was talk in Washington of what to do for Bush. His name surfaced to be the first administrator of the EPA, but he was batted down because of his ties to Big Oil. Unknown to Bush, his job opportunities were complicated by Nixon's determination to win over John Connally, the great enemy of the Texas Republican Party, as a way of drawing conservative Democrats nationally. Connally, whom Nixon intended to name as Treasury secretary, cautioned the president that some post would have to be found for Bush before the announcement to avoid even more political rancor in Texas. Alexander Haig, Henry Kissinger's deputy at the National Security Council, later recalled Kissinger's annoyance when he heard that the White House was considering Bush for the post of permanent representative to the United Nations. "*Vat* am I to do with this turkey?" Kissinger allegedly told Haig.

Bush did receive the UN job as a consolation prize, but only after Daniel Patrick Moynihan turned it down. At the United Nations Bush used his talents for listening and empathy to good effect. Aware that he knew little about foreign affairs, Bush crammed intensively. He even made a trip out to the Johnson ranch to seek LBJ's advice on foreign affairs.

The issue of China dominated Bush's first year in the job. One of the founding members of the United Nations, the Republic of China had held China's seat in the General Assembly and its veto power in the Security Council despite the victory of Mao Zedong's Communist revolution in 1949 and the displacement of Chiang Kai-shek's regime to the island of Taiwan. Ever since then, the United States had opposed the annual effort by the Communist members of the UN to unseat the Republic of China and replace it with the People's Republic of China. As Bush took his post, Nixon and Kissinger were secretly setting in motion a revolution in U.S. policy toward China. Not only was Bush not informed of Nixon's goal of visiting Beijing, but Kissinger actively misinformed him. In March 1971 Kissinger told Bush that "he had a strong feeling the State Department was maneuvering around to sell out Nationalist China down the line." Even after Nixon announced on July 15 that Kissinger had taken a secret trip to China and that he also planned to visit there, Bush was not given much guidance. "At this moment, I don't know what our China policy in the U.N. will turn out to be," Bush wrote in his diary four days later, "but all the U.N. people feel that the ball game is over, Peking is in and Taiwan is out." For the next three months Bush worked hard to prevent that prophecy from happening, hoping to secure the votes for a "two China" solution at the UN. In what would be a hard lesson in international diplomacy, Bush collected enough "promises" to support Taiwan that he was confident that the expulsion could be delayed for at least another year. However, it was not to be. "I still remember the countries that promised to vote for us and didn't," Bush later groused in his presidential campaign memoir. On October 24, 1971, the General Assembly voted 59–55 on a procedural vote that would prepare the way for Taiwan's expulsion.

The vote increased the tension with Kissinger, who was on his way to Beijing when the vote occurred. "I am not amused," Kissinger told Bush in an ugly telephone call after his return. "The source of his ire," Bush recalled for his diary, "seemed to be the fact that he felt I told him the vote would come later, towards October 28." Kissinger worried that domestic conservatives would blame him personally for Taiwan's defeat at the UN because the vote occurred while he was on a mission to court Mao.

Bush resented Kissinger's criticism. Throughout the fall he had been "plagued by the thought" that Nixon and Kissinger did not really want to win the China vote at the UN because they had cut "some side deal" with Beijing to make Nixon's visit possible. As the winning side jeered Taiwan at the UN, Bush made a point of walking out with the Nationalist Chinese delegate. "I think history will show the Nixon initiative to Peking is the thing that lost the U.N.," Bush wrote at the time. Although he considered the opening to China "a brilliant move," he was unhappy about the outcome at the UN, where a staunch U.S. ally had been sacrificed. "I had my heart and soul wrapped up in the policy of keeping Taiwan from being ejected. The withdrawal symptoms have been horrible," he wrote to a friend.

Bush, however, was a good soldier. He made a point of developing a rapport with the incoming delegation from mainland China, and, in fact, he drew praise for his ability to make friends with most delegations. In part it was because he took very seriously his responsibility, as chief American representative, for the security of the delegations in New York City. The early 1970s were a time of domestic terrorism that was directed at foreign diplomats. Soviet diplomats, in particular, were the targets of attacks by the Jewish Defense League, which used violence to demand legal Jewish emigration from the USSR. Bush made a point of personally visiting any Soviet diplomat who was attacked, and when Arab diplomats feared retribution after the Palestine Liberation Organization's murder of the Israeli athletes at the Munich games, Bush sought additional police protection for them and both he and Barbara Bush made house calls to reassure the Arab envoys and their families.

By the end of 1972 change was in the air in the Nixon administration, and Bush welcomed it. Disappointed by the performance of congressional Republicans in the 1972 election, Richard Nixon decided to install a new chairman of the Republican National Committee. Despite having won the biggest landslide in the electoral college (520 out of 538 votes), Nixon lacked any coattails. Democrats gained two seats in the Senate, bringing their total to fifty-six, and though the Republicans gained twelve seats in the House, they still remained deep in the minority. The current chairman, Senator

Bob Dole of Kansas, was to be removed—and his replacement was George Bush.

The offer to replace Dole came at a good time for Bush, who was ready to move on. He had been frustrated to learn that the permanent representative at the UN had little influence on U.S. foreign policy, and he had not gotten on well with Henry Kissinger. But Nixon had continued to groom Bush, occasionally calling his chief diplomat at the UN to congratulate him on a well-delivered speech or encourage him to make more. "This side of Nixon," Bush wrote admiringly in his diary, "is totally unknown to people." Bush had been keeping his domestic political network alive and was eager to begin putting it to work. He had several backers who were especially ambitious for him, including longtime Houston friends Robert Mosbacher and James A. Baker III. Indeed, in mid-1971 he had allowed his political allies to make him believe, briefly, that he had a shot at replacing Spiro Agnew on the ticket in 1972 (he didn't really), and he and his friends wondered whether he should run for governor of Texas. On the face of it, the RNC job offered enormous political opportunities for Bush. Unlike Dole, who had to balance the needs of his constituents and his Senate office, Bush could devote himself full-time to building the party and collecting chits for a future run for higher office.

But this was early 1973, and the Nixon presidency would soon implode. On June 17, 1972, five men had been arrested trying to install listening devices in the Watergate offices of the Democratic National Committee. These men turned out to have connections to the Committee to Re-Elect the President, an organization established by the White House to run Nixon's election bid outside of the RNC, and directly to the White House. These connections burst to the forefront in early 1973 when James McCord, one of the burglars, sent a letter to the judge presiding over his trial that indicated he had been told to keep his mouth shut by the White House.

Even before McCord's revelation, Bush had firsthand knowledge of the poisonous political environment fostered by the Nixon White House, having encountered stiff opposition when he asked for the Committee to Re-Elect's political database and for the leftover funds from the 1972 election. Once again Bush, as in the case of China, was not in the loop regarding the White House's priorities. President Nixon's chief of staff, H. R. "Bob" Haldeman, resisted sharing this information and this money because Nixon's goal was to build a new national conservative coalition. There was concern that Bush, who was more party-oriented, might help Republicans who were not fully in support of the president's agenda. Even more revealing to Bush was the political machinery that the White House had set up to deceive the public and the press. Under the guidance of Nixon's counselor Charles Colson, the White House regularly created false letter-writing campaigns using both White House and RNC resources. Articles or commentaries favorable to the president were mailed to thousands of Americans in an untraceable way. When the celebrated journalist Jack Anderson asked a question about one of these letter campaigns, Bush told Haldeman through an aide that he refused to lie about who had actually paid for the operation. "His position is that he *will not* be put in a position of lying," the White House staffer explained. Bush was concerned not so much about the operation as about what should be done if the RNC got caught. Haldeman's staffer agreed with Bush. "I disagree with the idea of creating elaborate cover stories to answer press inquiries. . . . I prefer the [press secretary Ron] Ziegler approach to press inquiries on subjects we prefer not answering—'No comment' or 'I don't know anything about it.' . . . I will attempt to work these mailing flaws out directly with Bush in the future."

Bush blamed this environment on the arrogance of the men around Nixon and not on the president himself. Since the early 1960s Bush had drawn upon Nixon for assistance and political advice. Besides his own father, Bush viewed Nixon as his most significant political mentor. Therefore a sense of loyalty and gratitude blinded Bush to what was happening around him. As a parade of Nixon's top aides began appearing before the Senate Watergate Committee, Bush recommended to Nixon that he make more public appearances. Convinced that Nixon was a victim, Bush assumed that through more personal contact Nixon could calm fears among fellow Republicans. Bush also wanted Nixon to consider reaching out to blacks and Mexican Americans. These suggestions were ignored.

The revelation in July 1973 that Richard Nixon had installed a secret taping system in the White House sparked a slow, painful process of reevaluation for Bush. The news a few months later that eighteen and a half minutes were found to be erased in a critical recording involving the president and Haldeman only increased Bush's doubts. "There is something unclear about all of this," he wrote. "There is something going on I don't know about, there's something either on the tapes or about the tapes that does not ring true to me." At risk was much more than Bush's opinion of Richard Nixon. As the most visible representative of the Republican Party after the president, Bush faced the prospect of being tarred with the widening Watergate scandal. He had not been in Washington in June 1972 and was blameless in the cover-up, but every day the White House expected him to defend the president's ever more tenuous explanations of his role in the scandal.

Although some of his friends suggested he consider resigning, Bush would not. The syndicated columnist Rowland Evans, who had been touting Bush's career since 1964 and had become a friend, had warned Bush "to get out before he drags you into the mud like everyone else he touches." Bush demurred, saying, "It's not a time to jump sideways, it's not a time for me to wring my hands on the sidelines." He waited until the spring of 1974 to start distancing the RNC and himself from the president. He told Alexander Haig, who by then had replaced Haldeman as chief of staff, that he had to be concerned about future elections and "the Party as well as the president, and they are not always in agreement."

George Bush was glad that his father was not around to witness "this grubby business." Prescott Bush had lost a short battle with lung cancer in the fall of 1972. The death of the man he had used as a yardstick to measure himself, the individual he called "my hero," left a hole in Bush's life. The loss of his father made Bush momentarily more desirous of Nixon's approval. In an emotionally wrenching letter to his sons in late July 1974, Bush revealed that he cared that the president considered him to be "soft, weak." "It stings but it doesn't bleed," he wrote. Even though he felt increasingly uncomfortable with Nixon, Bush believed that the president had been caricatured by the media and his political enemies and should not have to leave office.

After the "smoking gun" tape (which revealed Nixon to have schemed in June 1972 to use the CIA to block the FBI's Watergate investigation) was released on August 5, 1974, Bush changed his mind and reluctantly concluded that Nixon had to resign. On August 6 he sent a letter saying this to President Nixon, and then, at a cabinet meeting on August 7, Bush raised the issue of Watergate despite the fact that the president was trying to avoid discussing it. The next day Nixon announced his resignation, effective August 9.

Although the entire affair had revealed flaws in Bush's political antennae, the Watergate trauma did nothing to weaken his drive for higher office. Indeed, as the Nixon presidency collapsed, he saw an opportunity for political gain. The new president, Gerald R. Ford, would need a vice president. Led by James Baker, who quickly flew up to Washington, Bush's friends began to lobby for him as they had done in 1968. This time Bush was a serious contender, who figured at or near the top of short lists compiled by Ford's inner circle. But whispering about Bush's connection to the Townhouse operation hurt, as did a sense among some party leaders that Bush, though energetic and attractive, was an intellectual lightweight. When Ford called to say that he had chosen former New York governor Nelson Rockefeller instead, Bush was disappointed. "For valid reasons," Bush explained to Baker, "we made the finals . . . and so the defeat was more intense." With this loss, Bush entered a new category. No American politician had ever tried so hard to be vice president and failed.

Once again Bush received a consolation prize. Ford offered him a major European ambassadorship, but Bush surprised him by asking for China. And Ford agreed to make him the head of the two-year-old U.S. Liaison Office there. For years, whenever attempting to serve an ace on the tennis court, Bush would yell, "Unleash Chiang!" in reference to the anti-Communist slogan to let the Chinese Nationalists go after Mao. Now he was going to Red China.

China was a move sideways off the path to the White House, which Bush seemed to need after the struggles of Watergate. Kissinger continued to ignore him as he had at the United Nations, and most of Bush's efforts were designed to create a good rapport on the local level, with the Chinese and foreign diplomats. He set a precedent by using bicycles and attending events at foreign embassies, which his predecessor, the patrician David Bruce, had not attended. He also opened the U.S. mission to guests, serving them American fare and treating them to games.

The time there, however, was a rest stop. "Politics is always going to be a part of me," Bush had said at the time he went to China. From Beijing, Bush looked to opportunities at home. The year 1976 loomed as yet another chance to be a running mate.

In Washington, Ford wanted to shake up his cabinet. Bush was touted to replace the ailing Rogers Morton at the Commerce Department, with Elliott Richardson taking William Colby's spot as director of Central Intelligence. But those plans were displaced at the last moment. The two most plausible explanations, neither of which can yet be proved definitively, are that Bush was offered the CIA post instead because Henry Kissinger was vehemently opposed to the choice of Richardson or because Ford's chief of staff, the equally ambitious Donald Rumsfeld, feared that Bush might be a viable candidate for the vice presidency if Ford dumped Nelson Rockefeller in 1976. Making Bush the country's chief spymaster would presumably end his political future. In any event, Bush was given CIA and Richardson, Commerce.

For a man who had used presidential patronage to navigate his way to higher office, the CIA was an unwanted stepping-stone. Both George and Barbara Bush cried when they heard the offer. It seemed to them to mark the end of Bush's political career. No one had ever moved from the CIA, let alone from the director's office, to high elective office of any kind. If there was any doubt that taking the job would have negative political consequences, it was removed when Senator Frank Church of Idaho insisted that as part of Bush's confirmation, Gerald Ford forswear choosing Bush as his running mate in 1976. Yet Bush accepted the condition and agreed to the job.

In January 1976 George Bush took over an agency in crisis. A series of front-page stories a little over a year earlier by the *New York Times* journalist Seymour Hersh had revealed the CIA's involvement in assassination plots against foreign leaders and in monitoring student radicals at home. Coming in the wake of the sleazy political stories of Watergate, these articles led to congressional investigations, headed by Church in the Senate and later by Otis Pike in the House. By the end of 1975 President Ford had signed legislation establishing legislative oversight of the intelligence community and ending the code of "plausible deniability" that had protected presidents since 1947 from taking personal responsibility for any covert action initiated by the CIA.

"Bush's first speech in the Bubble [an auditorium built alongside the old CIA headquarters in Langley, Virginia] set the right tone," recalled John Waller, a longtime CIA officer who had started in the Office of Strategic Services in World War II and retired from the post of CIA inspector general in the 1980s. Bush called intelligence officers patriots—something few had been willing to do publicly in the wake of the revelations—and offered himself as a cheerleader for the service.

In his short tenure Bush witnessed the launch of the KH-11, the first spy satellite to transmit real-time photographs via relay stations to Washington, and broadened the key U.S. liaison with the British to include sharing this new satellite imagery. Meanwhile he put off the hard decisions about what to do with the aging cadre of intelligence professionals who had started their service in World War II and had become exhausted volcanoes and political liabilities. One decision Bush did not ignore, however, involved an escalating political issue.

Ever since the Soviets had surprised CIA analysts by testing four different strategic missile systems in 1973, the agency had undertaken some soul searching over how to explain Soviet intentions. As information about Soviet capabilities leaked to the public, conservatives used the agency's apparent surprise as a truncheon to criticize U.S. intelligence as being naive about the Kremlin. To calm foreign policy hawks and to instill some rigor into CIA analysis, Bush approved the unprecedented creation of an outside panel to provide a competitive estimate of the Soviet Union. Known as "Team B" when the exercise and the group's conclusions were leaked later in 1976, the group was headed by the Harvard professor Richard Pipes and included members of the Committee on the Present Danger, an independent pressure group that had lobbied against Kissinger and Nixon's effort to establish détente, or coexistence, with the Soviets. Rather than recognizing the Soviet Union as an economic basket case that was clinging to its nuclear program as a matter of prestige, the group described a Kremlin that not only was seeking military superiority and world domination but was primed to get both. Bush did not accept these conclusions and was furious when they leaked; nevertheless, the process gave credence to a particularly dark vision of the Soviet threat that people close to the far right, led now by Ronald Reagan, would soon tout. Among CIA professionals, however, Bush earned high praise for his handling of the Team B matter. By letting outsiders in, he had reduced pressures that might have forced a greater politicization of intelligence estimates.

During the 1976 presidential campaign Bush provided Jimmy Carter, the Democratic nominee, with intelligence briefings, as was standard practice. Meanwhile, Ford did indeed replace Rockefeller, but his choice as running mate was Bush's old rival Bob Dole. After Carter was elected, Bush offered to stay on for a few months, believing that the position of DCI should not be viewed as political. But Carter wanted his own director, settling on Admiral Stansfield Turner after it became clear that his first choice, the former Kennedy speechwriter and adviser Theodore C. Sorensen, would not be confirmed.

Bush then went back to Houston, where most pundits assumed the young-looking fifty-two-year-old would give up politics and be content amassing the fortune that most thought he already had. But they did not understand George Bush.

2

The Understudy

"There has [sic] been withdrawal symptoms," George Bush admitted to a friend in March 1977, six weeks after leaving Washington,
D.C. "I've been tense as a coiled spring hopefully not a shit about
it, but up tight . . . I just get bored silly about whose daughter is
a Pi Phi or even bored about whose [sic] banging Joe's wife. I don't
want to slip into that 3 to 4 martini late dinner rich social thing."
Despite admitting that it seemed "overwhelmingly presumptuous
and egotistical," he wasted no time in starting to think about running for president in 1980.

In the spring of 1978 George and Barbara Bush set off on a
round-the-world trip. Among the leaders they met was the shah of
Iran, who warned George Bush about Soviet intentions, especially
in Afghanistan. He also said that Iraq and Syria were both "a real
menace." Finally, the shah confessed his concerns about Jimmy
Carter's efforts to pressure his country to expand human rights.
Bush agreed, saying that the Democrats were applying this policy
selectively and undermining traditional U.S. allies. As the Bushes
left Iran they had no idea that the meeting with the shah would
be portentous of the future.

Once he came home from this fact-finding mission, Bush gathered some friendly congressmen and other advisers to discuss the
economy and other "big" domestic issues. It was no secret to his

friends that he was gearing up for the 1980 presidential election. Indeed, he was already thinking of running when Jimmy Carter invited him to witness Stansfield Turner's swearing in at CIA headquarters in early March 1977. A year later, he not only was sure he would throw his hat in the ring but was optimistic he could win. "I honestly believe I can do it," he related to Charles Guy, the friendly editor of a newspaper in Lubbock, Texas. Bush's longtime friend James Baker signed on to run Bush's political action committee, the Fund for Limited Government. Baker shared Bush's optimism, though he observed that at this point in the race George Bush was an asterisk in public opinion polls. To win, Baker suggested a strategy cribbed from Jimmy Carter's playbook. In 1976 the former governor of Georgia had used the early contests in Iowa and New Hampshire to catapult himself ahead of better-known candidates. Baker suggested that Bush, like Carter, go door-to-door in Iowa and New Hampshire and establish a personal connection with as many people as possible. Bush also planned to visit other states, too. Over the course of 1978 he would log 96,000 miles and visit forty-two of them.

From the moment Bush formally declared his candidacy at a Washington press conference in May 1979, it was clear that his campaign would be less about policy than about the man. To the extent he had a platform, it was reminiscent of his Senate race in 1970. On foreign policy, he seemed to be a hawk. He opposed Carter's SALT II arms control agreement with the Soviets, he opposed the Panama Canal Treaty that would hand the American-built canal to the Panamanians by 2000, and he opposed Carter's human rights policy. Domestically, however, there seemed to be no thread that held his views together. On the one hand, Bush appeared to be a civic or moderate Republican. He supported the Equal Rights Amendment, food stamps, and the planned-parenthood movement, and he opposed a constitutional ban on abortions, a "supply-side" across-the-board 30 percent cut in income taxes, and a balanced budget amendment. On the other hand, he endorsed oil deregulation and investment tax cuts and opposed federal funding for abortions. When asked why he was running, Bush recited a résumé instead of a rationale. He also spoke of his ambition and revealed more than a touch of arrogance. "There has to be a certain ego factor to drive a person to run for the Presidency," he told a reporter in 1979. "I've been driven to do a lot of things in life. I was driven to be a success in business, to excel in college, to be the youngest fighter pilot. I'm confident that I'm better than those other guys, but so far I haven't been able to prove it."

Ronald Reagan was unquestionably the front-runner in the Republican contest. In 1976 the former California governor and movie actor had fallen only sixty delegates shy of becoming the nominee. Confident that 1980 would be his year, Reagan's first campaign team (which would be replaced later) assumed that the governor needed only to pick up a few more delegates in the Northeast to win. While Bush had practically moved to Iowa, Reagan rarely visited the state, used a plane instead of a bus, and seemed of a mind to coast to victory.

Not even the most optimistic of Bush's team assumed the race would quickly become Reagan vs. Bush. Initially Reagan's most prominent opponent was the charismatic Texan John Connally, who had become a Republican after joining Nixon's cabinet and who entered the race with a lot of money to spend. Besides Connally the field included two senators, Minority Leader Howard Baker and Bob Dole, and two congressmen, the conservative Philip Crane and the liberal John Anderson.

Thanks to an excellent organization—some of which Bush had been building for a decade—an estimated million pieces of mail, and his tireless campaigning, Bush catapulted himself to the head of the field by upsetting Reagan in the Iowa precinct caucuses, winning 33 percent of the vote to 30 percent for Reagan. Delighting the media with his garbled patrician syntax, Bush proclaimed his "Big Mo," which would prove short-lived. The success in Iowa made the Bush team overconfident in New Hampshire. Instead of waiting a few more months to characterize this as a two-man race, they started acting as if the other candidates did not exist. This set up the blunder that ended any real hopes for Bush in 1980. The Bush campaign jumped when Reagan's key operative in the state suggested a face-to-face debate in Nashua and then secured the *Nashua Telegraph* as a sponsor. When Bob Dole complained that by not inviting the rest of the field the *Nashua Telegraph* was effectively making an illegal contribution to the Reagan and Bush campaigns, the Federal Election Commission agreed. So the two campaigns began discussing splitting the cost of the debate; but then Bush decided not to contribute anything because there had been a deal. After deciding to pick up the whole tab, the Reagan camp concluded it would be a mistake to enhance Bush's stature by making it a two-man debate. Quietly, Reagan's people called the other candidates and invited them to participate.

George Bush realized what was going on only when the other candidates—Anderson, Baker, Crane, and Dole (Connally had already taken his campaign south)—showed up at the Nashua High School gymnasium. Bush's reaction became a defining moment. When Bush refused to participate in a six-man debate, Reagan stormed out from behind the curtain with the other candidates in tow. The local organizer then called for Reagan's microphone to be turned off, to which Reagan bellowed what would be the catchphrase of the 1980 primaries: "I paid for this microphone, Mr. Green." (The man's name was Breen, but Reagan had made his point.) Cameras caught Bush saying nothing and staring ahead like a deer caught in the headlights. As one wag noted, "He looked like a boy who had been dropped off at the wrong birthday party." Bush's numbers had already been declining after an earlier debate with Reagan in Manchester, but it was his paralysis on the stage in Nashua that wiped out his front-runner status for good.

Bush's political career might well have disappeared in the spring of 1980 with the snows of Nashua. But he stayed in the race and became a better campaigner. He won a handful of New England primaries but then surprised analysts by winning in Pennsylvania and Michigan. In Pennsylvania he offered himself as the anti-Reagan candidate, coining the term *voodoo economics* to describe the governor's plans for cutting taxes, increasing defense spending, and balancing the budget. The Michigan victory came after former president Gerald Ford ended any speculation that he might lead a last-minute effort to deny Reagan the nomination and let it be known that he wanted Bush to be the alternative to Reagan.

Within the Bush campaign, however, there was concern that if he did not pull out soon, he would lose any chance at being Ronald Reagan's running mate. Ironically, the one job Bush had ever campaigned for before, the vice presidency, was slipping away from him because he enjoyed running hard for the top slot. And so, for the candidate's own good, Baker forced Bush to get out, pulling the plug on the eve of the California primary by saying the campaign lacked the funds to compete there. Bush, annoyed, let it be known that he was still undecided, but the end was inevitable.

What was not inevitable was that he would be chosen as Ronald Reagan's number two. According to the Reagan biographer Lou Cannon, the Reagan campaign was prepared to select George Bush for the second spot before the candidate himself was ready to do so. Ronald Reagan harbored doubts about Bush's political instincts, not simply because he had stayed in the race so long but also because of how he had handled the Nashua debate. Bush, he told aides, "just melts under pressure." Bush struck him as remarkably thin-skinned for a politician. Reagan also hoped that he might be able to entice former president Gerald Ford to be his running mate. It was not unprecedented for a former president to return to public life; John Quincy Adams represented Massachusetts in the House of Representatives and William Howard Taft served as chief justice of the United States Supreme Court. But no former president had ever served as vice president. Reagan broached the idea with Ford privately in June 1980 and, though he wasn't sure how it would work out, asked Ford to consider it. Reluctant at first, by the time of the July convention in Detroit, Ford had deputized a team led by Henry Kissinger and the economist Alan Greenspan to talk to Reagan's team, led by the campaign chairman William Casey. The negotiations touched on a share of responsibilities, with Ford perhaps taking the lead on foreign policy, but never reached a final plan before Gerald Ford spoiled the magic. In an interview with Walter Cronkite, Ford revealed that he was being courted for the vice presidency and was considering it, so long as he "would not be a figurehead vice president." Once Reagan saw the interview, he knew that this "dream team" would not work. He had to be his own president. And with the Ford option off the table, he chose Bush, feeling that he had to go with the man who had won the second largest number of delegates.

When news of the negotiations with Ford first reached Bush, gloom descended on his camp. He did not expect to be chosen for the ticket. Meanwhile his delegates were planning to push his agenda against the Reaganites: pro–equal rights amendment and pro-choice. And Bush resigned himself to giving the Houston social and business community a second try. Then the call came. Reagan did not go into specifics but asked whether Bush felt he could support his platform. Bush agreed, once more performing the trick of the political chameleon. He was a Goldwater Republican again. It had been sixteen years since he had presented himself as a man of the hard Right, but he knew how to do it. Bush had his supporters put their ERA signs away, and he announced his personal opposition to abortion.

·   ·   ·

Reagan's decisive election over Jimmy Carter in November 1980 gave Bush the job he had been dreaming about since the late 1960s.

The hard part for Bush was to make the job worth the effort. He planned to be loyal. "I will keep a low profile," he told one interviewer, "and I will not have hurt feelings when people ask, 'What happened to George Bush?'" Yet, at the same time, Bush admitted to another interviewer, "What I want is for people to wake up in two years and say, 'You know, this guy did something.'" Bush wished to model his vice presidency after that of his predecessor, Walter Mondale, whom Jimmy Carter had involved in the policy process. Initially, it was thanks to his friend James Baker that this was possible. Baker had so impressed and cultivated the Reagans, especially Nancy Reagan, during the fall campaign that he was given the post of White House chief of staff. This was a critical development because Bush would need access to alter Reagan's opinion of him and to have a chance to be a player in this administration. Soon Bush was being invited to Reagan's morning national security briefings, and he and the president began a weekly Thursday luncheon. More significant, Baker arranged for members of his staff to brief Bush regularly on domestic affairs. And when the incoming secretary of state, Alexander Haig, declared himself the "Vicar of Foreign Policy" and seemed to be pushing himself too far forward, Bush was chosen by the White House to clip Haig's wings. He, and not Haig, was selected to chair the National Security Council's Crisis Management Center, and then the National Security Planning Group, which established foreign policy options for Reagan.

But what most caused a sea change in Reagan's impression of Bush was how the vice president responded to the attempt on Reagan's life on March 30, 1981. Bush had begun the day in Houston, where he was to give some speeches, and did not expect fate to intervene. In Washington Reagan was exiting the ballroom of the Washington Hilton Hotel, where he had just given a luncheon speech to the Construction Trades Council, when he was shot by John Hinckley Jr.

As the president underwent surgery and Bush hurried back

from Texas, the Reagan administration gave the image of a government in chaos. Al Haig's blustery effort to calm the international media by proclaiming, "I'm in charge," and then by implying, wrongly, that he was next in the line of succession after the traveling vice president, had the exact opposite effect.

Bush, however, surprised Reagan's inner circle by exhibiting both great tact and nerves of steel. He pointedly overruled suggestions that to speed his return he take a helicopter to the South Lawn of the White House. At 7:00 P.M., four and half hours after the shooting, Bush entered the White House Situation Room. When told that the Dairy Price Support Bill was awaiting Reagan's signature and that the deadline was the following day, Bush said that the decision could wait another twenty-four hours to see how the president felt then. After asking Defense Secretary Caspar Weinberger for a report on the status of Soviet forces, and being assured that the situation there was normal, Bush turned to the possibility of using the military to assist the family of James Brady, the gravely wounded press secretary, in bringing them from Chicago where they were having trouble getting seats on a commercial carrier. "Let's try to keep everything as normal as possible, including the scheduling," said Bush, who agreed to take Reagan's national security briefing the next morning and to meet the Dutch prime minister, who happened to be in town. Bush even felt so comfortable in his role as crisis manager that he overruled James Baker, who had suggested that there not be a meeting of the cabinet because it would draw attention to the absence of the president. The vice president disagreed. He wanted to use the meeting to convey the message that the U.S. government was still working. And he told the members of the crisis team that to maintain public trust it was also important "to level with the American people and give them full and accurate information."

Bush successfully played the role of crisis manager more than once. He remained the chair when the crisis management center became the Special Situations Group. In October 1983 when the United States prepared to invade Grenada to overthrow a pro-Cuban Marxist regime and rescue one thousand Americans resident on the Caribbean island, he coordinated activities in the White House because Reagan and Haig's replacement as secretary of state, George Shultz, were in Augusta, Georgia. But in the first term it was never clear whether Bush's views actually shaped the foreign policy decisions made. In February 1984, a few months after the Shiite terrorist group Hezbollah had killed 241 U.S. servicemen at the Beirut airport, Bush sided with those who argued for removing the remaining American troops from Lebanon. Until the last moment, when Reagan finally agreed, the president had been wavering.

Bush was happy not to reveal when, if ever, he disagreed with Reagan's foreign policy. On domestic policy, where Bush's policy preferences were not as strong, he certainly had his doubts. He was never fully won over by supply-side economics. Nevertheless, when a prominent Republican senator advised him in late 1981 to "separate yourself from the President" on the deficit issue, he refused. In a letter to Richard Nixon—with whom Bush had reestablished a relationship—he explained, "I don't believe a President should have to be looking over his shoulder wondering if the Vice President was out there carving him up or undermining his programs in one way or another." Nixon, himself a former vice president, had written to Bush sympathetically.

In Reagan's 1984 reelection campaign, Bush's performance was uneven; even his strong performances came in for criticism. After debating the Democratic vice presidential nominee, Geraldine Ferraro, Bush celebrated, saying that he had whipped "some ass," which many saw as disrespectful to the first woman to have ever been on a major party ticket. Even so, after the landslide election victory over Walter Mondale, Bush's role in the administration, especially in foreign policy, remained significant. Beginning in 1985, the number of people attending Reagan during his early morning national security briefing was four: National Security Adviser Robert MacFarlane, Bush, and Reagan's new chief of staff, Donald Regan.

As a result, over the course of the next two years, Bush became a key participant in the two most controversial foreign policies of the Reagan era. He shared Reagan's concern that the 1979 Marxist revolution in Nicaragua had made all of Central America vulnerable to Soviet, Cuban, and Nicaraguan machinations. When the U.S. Congress placed restraints on funding the counterrevolutionary guerrillas in Nicaragua, the Contras, Bush lent his support to finding private sources of funding. Meanwhile Reagan assigned Bush a leading role in shaping the administration's counterterrorism policy. After the high-profile hijacking in June 1985 of a TWA airliner, which was commandeered to Beirut, the administration formed the Task Force on Combatting Terrorism, for which Bush became the chair. "Bush was not viewed as having any institutional stake," recalled Admiral John Poindexter, who was then Robert MacFarlane's deputy. Indeed U.S. counterterrorism in the Reagan years had been marked by a struggle between the hawkish Secretary of State Shultz and a secretary of defense, Caspar Weinberger, who was reluctant to use force against largely invisible terrorist groups.

As Bush's task force met, the vice president participated in high-level discussions over how to alter the behavior of the world's acknowledged leader in supporting terrorism, Iran. Since March 1984, Iranian-sponsored terrorists had been kidnapping Americans in Lebanon. As of the summer of 1985, seven Americans were held hostage, and there seemed to be no way to free them. With U.S. intelligence information too fragmentary to permit a rescue mission, and Ronald Reagan emotionally committed to doing something for these people, a small group within the administration considered an innovative solution. An Israeli proposition that the United States assist in currying favor with Iranian moderates through selling arms to the Iranian government seemed to offer dual advantages. First, it would give the United States a foot in the door to alter the character of Iranian foreign policy once the country's octogenarian supreme leader, Ayatollah Ruhollah Khomeini, died. Second, the Iranians might put pressure on their clients in Lebanon to release the foreign hostages. MacFarlane saw this as the big play, analogous to Nixon's opening to China in 1971–72.

The precise nature of Bush's thinking on the Iranian gambit remains shrouded in historical mist because many documents from that period remain classified. There is already strong publicly available evidence, however, that though he may have had some quibbles, he supported the main thrust of the policy of selling arms to the Iranians for strategic and tactical gains even though this would clash with his task force's recommendations on how to handle terrorist groups. There is even stronger evidence that due to his importance in the administration, he was one of the few in a position to prevent the policy from occurring. Remarkably, the sometime rivals Shultz and Weinberger both opposed the policy, and Bush's support of them—had he agreed with them—might have tipped the balance.

After the Reagan administration sanctioned Israeli sales of nearly 500 TOW missiles and 185 HAWK missiles—the president had signed a document on December 5, 1985, "finding" this covert operation to have been in the U.S. national interest—the policy came up for review on December 7. Having already accepted an invitation to attend the Army-Navy game, Bush called John Poindexter, who had replaced MacFarlane as national security adviser earlier in the year, to ask whether he should skip the game to attend the meeting. Poindexter, who was a major proponent of going ahead, told him not to worry. The implication was that Bush's vote was not needed. Shultz and Weinberger's opposition would not derail the policy.

Reagan went ahead with the next phase of the covert Iran initiative without informing Shultz and Weinberger. On January 6 Bush and Chief of Staff Regan were with Poindexter when Reagan signed another draft finding for the initiative. Had any of these men been against it, they could have asked the president to wait for a formal meeting of his national security team on January 7, where Shultz and Weinberger presumably would have put up resistance. None of them protested that Admiral Poindexter was using a briefing as a way to implement a controversial policy decision.

The only known reluctance expressed by Bush—which he shared with the Tower Commission later established to investigate what became known as the Iran-Contra scandal—was that since U.S. and Israeli interests were not identical, the Israelis should be cut out of the operation. On January 17, in the presence of Poindexter, Regan, and Bush, President Reagan signed another finding that did just that. The United States would now sell 3,504 TOW missiles directly to Iran, in violation of a U.S. law prohibiting military sales to countries on the Department of State's terrorism list. Neither Weinberger nor Shultz was told about this presidential finding, either. Ultimately Hezbollah would release three American hostages and would seize three more to replenish its supply. Reagan and Bush were caught in a hostage mill.

Thus did Bush become one of the key officials responsible for the dismantling of Reagan's National Security Council structure. As the Tower Commission found, "Thereafter, the only senior-level review the Iran initiative received was during one or another of the President's daily national security briefings. These were routinely attended only by the President, the Vice President, Mr. Regan and VADM [Vice Admiral] Poindexter." And this occurred at the same moment when Bush's task force issued a report suggesting improvements to the country's counterterrorism capabilities and decrying ever paying ransom to terrorists. The gap between stated policy and the administration's activities would not stay secret long.

· · ·

The midterm elections of 1986 were the last of the Reagan era, and Bush's thoughts naturally turned to the 1988 presidential contest. Bush marked this event by starting his own campaign diary. "Why do you want to be president?" he wrote on November 5. Ironically, the first entry of the diary also noted an event that would metastasize into a major threat to those presidential hopes. That day wire services carried a report from a Lebanese newspaper, *Al Shiraa*, that the U.S. government was sending arms to Iran and negotiating for the release of the hostages held by Hezbollah. "I'm one of the few people that know fully the details," Bush confided to his diary, "and there is a lot of flak and misinformation out there. It is not a subject we can talk about."

As knowledge of the Iranian initiative seeped out, there was widespread criticism of the administration for what seemed to be a ploy to trade arms for hostages. Sensitive to their effect on his own political future, Bush initially sought to downplay the rumors. On November 7 Bush went on television to say that it was "inconceivable" that the United States was engaged in such activity. Not only was this a bald-faced lie; it was the beginning of a cover-up.

Bush's concern was that the lie would not hold because of George Shultz. On November 9 Bush's close friend former senator Nicholas Brady of New Jersey called Shultz to take his political temperature. In return, Brady got a warning from Shultz that Bush's incautious comments were about to get him into trouble. "If he blows his integrity, he's finished," Shultz said to Brady, referring to Bush. "He should be very careful how he plays the 'loyal lieutenant role' now."

But Bush was doing more than being loyal to Reagan. He was trying to protect himself. The next day Bush invited Shultz and his wife to dinner. Shultz now warned Bush directly not to lie in public about the policy. Bush was furious and told Shultz to keep in mind that there had been larger strategic objectives involved in making the approach to Iran. "You can't be technically right; you have to be right," replied Shultz. "There was considerable tension between us when we parted," Shultz later noted.

Bush knew that as Shultz's opposition to the Iran operation had become apparent, the secretary of state had been cut out by Donald Regan, John Poindexter, and himself. "Indeed, he [Shultz] had felt cut out," Bush noted in his diary the night after their confrontation. "And, he was dealing from less than a full deck on the Iran situation." Bush worried that Shultz would resign and cause a public furor.

Meanwhile the National Security Council staff prepared a chronology of what had happened, a chronology that was false, omitting what Regan, Poindexter, and Bush knew to be the truth of the deliveries via the Israelis in mid-1985. Believing that the Iranians were on the verge of releasing two more American hostages, Regan, Bush, and Poindexter agreed that there should not be any presidential statement on this at all. But the unity of this inner group was breaking down. Donald Regan no longer agreed with trying to maintain public silence. "We getting murdered in Press," Regan noted in his own diary. "I want to go public. Pres, VP & JP saying no—too risky."

The inner group also wanted Shultz and Weinberger to agree to a statement that "there was unanimous support for the President's decision." When Shultz disagreed vehemently, saying, "That's a lie. It's Watergate all over again," Bush and Poindexter changed their strategy for dealing with the expanding crisis. Reagan would speak to the American people on the Iran matter, but Bush, Poindexter, and Donald Regan decided that the president's statement would have to be misleading about the role played by the Israelis in the early shipments.

Fortunately for Poindexter and Bush, the befuddled Reagan had actually forgotten what he knew about the initial Israeli sales. He relied heavily on his own diary to remind him of what he knew, and there was little on this subject in his entries for the summer of 1985. Entries from the fall of 1985, however, made clear that in Reagan's mind the Iran initiative was inspired by a desire to free the U.S. hostages in Beirut. So when Reagan gave speeches on November 13, 1986, and again on November 19 denying the nature of what his government had been trying to do with Iran since August of the previous year, Reagan was, at best, telling half-truths. Vice President Bush, however, knew better.

The crisis entered a far more dramatic phase a few days later after an internal investigation led by Attorney General Edwin Meese discovered that the United States had overcharged the Iranians for the TOW missiles and had diverted some of the profits to aid the Contras. Poindexter resigned, and one of his assistants, Lieutenant Colonel Oliver North, whose name was on a memo about the diversion, was fired. A scandal that had involved a debate over the wisdom of ransom instantly acquired the hint of presidential impeachment. Did Reagan know that his aides were breaking the law forbidding lethal aid to the Contras? And for those looking to 1988, an equally important question was: did Bush know?

Bush, who liked Poindexter and made a point of visiting him in his office on his last day in the White House, wanted to avoid also being swallowed up in the scandal. When an independent prosecutor was later put on the case, Bush offered to take a lie detector test to show that he was ignorant of the diversion. Nevertheless, Bush was terrified that his chance at the presidency was in mortal danger because of his heavy involvement in U.S. foreign policy. In a cold-blooded move, he turned on Shultz and the one remaining man in the White House who had known as much about the Iran initiative as he had, Donald Regan. On November 25, 1986, he told the president, "I really felt that Regan should go, Shultz should go, and that he ought to get this all behind him in the next couple of months." On December 5 he again told President Reagan that it was time he considered firing his chief of staff. "I'm not of that mind," Reagan confessed to his diary. The evening before, the president had heard the same advice from his former close aide Michael Deaver, Nixon's former secretary of state Bill Rogers, and Robert Strauss, the longtime Democratic wise man, who was held in high esteem on both sides of the political divide. Bush, who knew these men, had probably heard of their advice.

This wasn't the first time Bush had tried to get Regan fired. Even before the Iran-Contra scandal blew up, he had gone to see Nancy Reagan privately in the White House residence. "I didn't want to say this on the phone," Bush reportedly told the first lady, "but I think Don should resign." Nancy Reagan said that she agreed but added, "I wish you'd tell my husband. I can't be the only one who's saying this to him." Gently refusing, Bush replied, "Nancy, that's not my role." Now, with Iran-Contra swirling, Bush believed that he had no choice.

Bush shaped Reagan's handling of the mess once Poindexter left. On December 3 Bush gave a speech to the American Enterprise Institute that became the boilerplate for a more thoughtful explanation of what had happened. Bush stated that he supported the administration's policy on Iran, though he did not indicate that he had been one of the key participants in shaping the policy. He then allowed that "mistakes were made" by the National Security Council staff in arranging for the illegal diversion of funds to the Contras, though Bush denied knowing anything about that. Bush also denied that Reagan believed he was ever trading arms for hostages, again without saying whether he himself had believed this. Both Reagan and former president Gerald Ford thought Bush had done well with his speech. Reagan would repeat the same phrases in his own defense of the policy given a few weeks later.

Memories of Watergate weighed heavily on Bush. Like Shultz, he worried about the parallels with Iran-Contra. The lesson of Watergate appeared to be that there could not be any cover-up of criminal behavior. Initially Bush had hoped that the Reagan administration could cover up the Iran operation, which he believed did not involve any criminal activity, but within a few days that became impossible. Once the Iran story was linked to the Contra issue, Bush understood that he and the president had to say more.

Iran-Contra remained a millstone on Bush's neck. He did not reveal his diary entries to the Tower Commission, to the Joint Congressional Committee impaneled to investigate the scandal, or to the Office of the Independent Counsel hired by the Department of Justice. Indeed, when Bush learned that Shultz had turned over his notes, he wrote in his diary: "Howard Baker in the presence of the President, told me today that George Shultz had kept 700 pages of personal notes, dictated to his staff . . . Notes on personal meetings he had with the President. I found this almost inconceivable. Not only that he kept the notes, but that he'd turned them all over to Congress . . . I would never do it. I would never surrender such documents and I wouldn't keep such detailed notes."

Bush made sure that no investigator saw his diary before the 1988 election. Two weeks after hearing that Shultz had turned over his diary, Bush misled the veteran *Washington Post* political reporter David Broder, saying, "If I had sat there and heard George Shultz and Cap [Caspar Weinberger] express it [their opposition to the Iran policy] strongly, maybe I would have had a stronger view. But when you don't know something, it's hard to react . . . We were not in the loop."

The biggest problem for Bush was not that he had managed the diversion but that his involvement in the Iran project revealed flaws in his own understanding of foreign policy. Like Robert MacFarlane, he had been seduced into believing that the secret opening to Iran was just as wise as Nixon's opening to China—which by itself revealed a deep misunderstanding of international affairs. In 1971 Henry Kissinger had been negotiating with Zhou Enlai, the Chinese premier, not with arms dealers out for profit. Moreover, the United States and the Chinese had a common enemy—the Soviet Union—and neither side expected payment to establish the dialogue. Iran and Hezbollah had played Reagan and Bush for fools.

Iran-Contra dealt a blow to Bush's hopes to model his 1988 campaign on Nixon's triumphant march to the Republican nomination in 1960, in which a vice president had run as a "semi-incumbent" and never relinquished the status of front-runner. The vice president's advisers scrambled to distance Bush from the burgeoning scandal and thus came up with a strategy in early 1987 to revive the terrorism task force to remind the public that Bush took the issue seriously. Impaneled rapidly, the task force then gave itself a grade on what had been accomplished in a year. The task force was hardly noticed, and those who did notice it were merely reminded that either Bush's views had been ignored by Reagan or he was a hypocrite when he argued against paying blackmail to terrorists.

Bush had no doubt that he wished to be elected president. He had worked so hard for so long, had taken so many difficult, politically unhelpful jobs from so many presidents, that he felt it was now his turn. But what platform would he run on? In the nearly quarter century since his first run for federal office, Bush had yet to fashion for himself a political program. He had coexisted with three major Republican leaders, Goldwater, Nixon, and Reagan, each of whom saw the world differently, and Bush had served each of them loyally.

Many observers considered Bush's political adaptability a sign of weakness. The same week in October 1987 that he announced his candidacy—this time in Houston, not in Washington, as he had done in 1979—Bush was rocked by a *Newsweek* cover story, headlined "Fighting the Wimp Factor." No one questioned the physical courage of this World War II veteran and eternally young tennis player and jogger. It was his political courage that was in question. The attack would not have stung so much if Bush himself did not, at times, question what others thought of his strength. What the article did not do was alter Bush's long-standing dislike of the press. This was the second damaging piece from *Newsweek*. Three months earlier, a reporter for the magazine had been asking questions about persistent rumors that Bush had had an affair with his longtime assistant Jennifer Fitzgerald. Unwisely, the vice president's eldest son, George W. Bush, had answered that question directly: "The answer to the Big A question is N-O," which spawned stories about a campaign that protested too much.

An opportunity arose in 1987 for Bush to move away from Reagan and identify himself with the more pragmatic conservatism of Richard Nixon and Gerald Ford that he had espoused as a congressman. In an effort to provide political cover for the next occupant of the White House—Democrat or Republican—Governor Mario Cuomo of New York (himself a potential Democratic nominee) had recommended a bipartisan commission on the budget. It was undeniable that whoever became president in January 1989 would face a daunting challenge. The passage of the Gramm-Rudman-Hollings bill in 1985 (revised in 1987) mandated a steady reduction in the budget deficit to zero by 1991. Deficit projections for the 1990 fiscal year, which would begin in October 1989, suggested that Congress would likely overshoot the deficit target, thus requiring draconian across-the-board spending cuts. What Congressman Bush would have supported in 1967, Vice President Bush rejected twenty years later. The presidential brass ring was tantalizingly close, and it seemed that fiscal responsibility would not give it to him. When Cuomo brought his idea to Bush in September 1987, he rejected it. "Wouldn't it be a tax increase commission?" Bush reportedly replied. Cuomo said the commission would have to make up its collective mind, but the problem of the deficit had to be taken out of politics and addressed. "Mr. Vice President, if you are fortunate enough to be president, you will not be able to do what you have to do without something like this." Bush not only disliked the idea but tried to kill it. He issued a press release saying that "in an election period, this matter isn't something for a commission to decide—it's something for voters to decide."

By contrast, Bush's likely rival for the Republican nomination, Senate majority leader Bob Dole, understood that the Cuomo idea would provide fiscal conservatives with a way out of the political appeal of a hard no-tax line. He supported the formation of the commission, which later included on the Republican side Senator Pete Domenici of New Mexico and former defense secretaries Caspar Weinberger and Donald Rumsfeld, and saw that it was attached as a rider to a budget bill. Bush and Dole both understood that Reagan had overseen twelve tax increases in his time in office, but the master politician had managed to push the blame elsewhere. Each took different lessons from that.

The Bush team's coronation strategy did not survive its first political test. As expected, the vice president lost the Iowa precinct caucuses to Dole (from neighboring Kansas), but Bush was not supposed to come in third. The surprisingly strong second-place showing by the television evangelist Pat Robertson, who took 25 percent to Dole's 37 percent and Bush's 19 percent, revealed cracks in the Reaganite coalition that Bush would need to mend if he was to have a chance of being the Republican nominee, let alone elected president. Crestfallen and anxious, Bush and his advisers tore up their schedules and hustled to New Hampshire, where the first primary was a week away. "I was born in Massachusetts, grew up in Connecticut, live across the way . . . in Maine and understand New Hampshire," Bush said in search of votes. "I'm one of you," he pleaded. But antitax New Hampshire's favorite remained Ronald Reagan, even though he was not running again. As Bush's twenty-point lead over Dole in the state vanished practically overnight after Iowa, he made a fateful decision to salvage his campaign.

As he had done in 1964 when he briefly turned his back on his family's commitment to civil rights, and in 1980 when he repudiated his own moderate views on social issues, George Bush sought to eliminate any remaining doubt that he would reject traditional Republican fiscal responsibility in order to get elected. The candidate retooled his stump speech to eliminate what few slivers of light he had allowed between himself and the sitting president and to heighten any differences with Dole. Dole had been the cosponsor of legislation establishing the bipartisan National Economic Commission, which would look at ways by which to eliminate the budget deficit. Dole had also been a major player in the economic summit of the fall, which, coming in the wake of the stock market crash of October 1987, had engineered a slightly smaller deficit through a combination of spending cuts and modest tax increases. On the stump after Iowa, Dole announced his commitment to a one-year budget freeze to stop the hemorrhaging while giving the next president the time to see what combination of actions could bring the budgetary outflows in line with revenues. These efforts by Dole, who was himself no economic progressive, reflected the thinking of the remaining civic Republicans who had never accepted the pie-in-the-sky assumptions of supply-side economists.

Bush responded with a pledge not to raise taxes of any kind. And to temper criticisms that he had no deficit-reduction strategy of his own, Bush offered the concept of the *flexible freeze*, an approach that held most spending at current levels (with a cost-of-living adjustment) and permitted some innovative spending on child care and the environment while keeping below the deficit targets mandated by Gramm-Rudman. When pressed on how this would work, Bush's economic advisers explained that the deficit would disappear by 1992 so long as the economy kept growing at between 2 and 3 percent a year and the interest rate dropped at least 2 points. In other words, there could be no recession or inflation, no war, no major natural disaster, or no collapse in the country's already fragile banking industry. To ensure that voters understood the difference between him and Dole, Bush then authorized political advertising that characterized the Kansan as "Senator Straddle" on this and other issues.

The new approach had impressive short-term benefits. Bush scored an eleven-percentage-point victory in the New Hampshire primary, restoring the image of political inevitability and fatally wounding Dole's candidacy. Bush understood that the victory was not simply the product of his new harsher antitax rhetoric. The Bush effort in New Hampshire, led by the state's pugnacious governor, John Sununu, had been extremely impressive. But Bush also learned from this experience that the Republican rank and file's loyalty to him was thin. He thus became essentially a single-issue candidate. Meanwhile Dole hurt himself by flashing some of the anger that had cost the Ford-Dole ticket votes in 1976. "Stop lying about my record," Dole glowered at Bush during a nationally telecast interview on the night of the New Hampshire primary. It was all downhill from there for the Kansas senator.

Victories in sixteen out of the seventeen "Super Tuesday" primaries in the South ensured Bush's nomination. The spadework of John Sununu in New Hampshire was matched by the efforts in the South of Lee Atwater, Bush's South Carolina–born campaign manager. Atwater had helped move Bush to court evangelicals and younger fans of stock car racing. Bush stopped talking about Kennebunkport, sported cowboy boots, and reminded listeners of his love of country music and his Texas hunting license.

The Democrats took six weeks longer to embrace a candidate. By April the field had narrowed to three men: Massachusetts governor Michael Dukakis, Senator Al Gore of Tennessee, and the civil rights icon Jesse Jackson. The front-runner Dukakis, who claimed credit for the "Massachusetts Miracle" of economic revitalization, promised a tougher, more business-oriented and pragmatic liberalism; Gore, a Vietnam veteran who had focused on national security issues in the Senate, touted the need for his leadership qualities in the Cold War and his domestic pragmatism; and Jackson appealed to those Democrats who still believed in Lyndon Johnson's Great Society. Dukakis had become the presumptive nominee by overwhelmingly defeating Congressman Richard Gephardt of Missouri in New Hampshire, by staying competitive with Gore and Jackson in the southern primaries and picking up some victories out west, and then by beating them in New York's delegate-rich contest on April 19.

Although little known outside the Northeast, and a plodding speaker who offered not much more than competence as a vision, Dukakis emerged as a serious challenger because of Bush's political vulnerability. The public seemed tired of the Reagan administration and was associating Bush with its proliferating scandals. Bush appeared to have direct links to the Panamanian strongman General Manuel Noriega, who in February had been indicted in absentia by a Miami court for drug smuggling. Noriega, a longtime CIA asset, had met with Bush when the latter was director of Central Intelligence in 1976 and again when he was vice president in 1983. By mid-May Bush was trailing Dukakis by sixteen percentage points. "How an incumbent vice president who wrapped up his party's nomination in March can be an underdog is amazing to me," commented Reagan's 1984 campaign manager, Ed Rollins.

As his campaign entered its second crisis of the year, Bush received a lot of advice and wavered. Some of his advisers, moderate Republicans, said, "Let Bush be Bush rather than Reagan's vice president," arguing that he should separate himself from President Reagan. Richard Nixon, whom the Bushes invited to a quiet dinner at their residence, agreed. The former president suggested Bush announce that he would fire the entire Reagan cabinet, an action, he argued, that would show that "you *are* a tough, no-nonsense administrator who isn't afraid to take bold actions even though you may break some china in the process." Some members of Bush's inner circle felt the same way. His aides inserted language into a speech he gave in Los Angeles that revealed his unhappiness that Reagan was considering a Shultz plan to offer Noriega a deal that would vacate his indictment if he promised to leave power. Bush, however, refused to reveal his differences with the president on a national security matter of even greater significance. A year earlier Bush had unsuccessfully argued within the administration that any agreement with the Soviets on eliminating intermediate-range nuclear missiles should permit both sides to retain one hundred nuclear warheads. Bush thought it prudent for the United States to have some of these missiles in Alaska. But Reagan, who believed that the world would be better off without any nuclear missiles, preferred an agreement that eliminated all of them on both sides. In May 1988, as the U.S. Senate was debating the ratification of the Intermediate-Range Nuclear Forces (INF) Treaty, Bush chose to keep his concerns on this matter to himself.

Meanwhile Barbara Bush recommended that the vice president visit an AIDS clinic—which he did days later—to show his compassion for the victims of that terrible disease. This offered a pointed contrast to Reagan, who had been reluctant to issue any public comment about the AIDS crisis and gave his only national address on the crisis in May 1987, even though it was a significant public health issue throughout most of his years in office.

Others, especially Lee Atwater, believed the key to Bush's success was not to move away from Reagan, but to attack Dukakis personally.

Nixon, who caught wind of Atwater's advice, tried to discourage Bush from taking the low road. "You will be urged by a number of your well-intentioned advisors to be more combative, to be a fighter, to sound strong, to show passion. Don't do it," he advised. "Anyone who tries to show strength by a strong voice and strong gestures conveys the opposite impression. The best way to convey a sense of strength on television is quiet control of power." Nixon suggested he allow surrogates to expose Dukakis as "a left-wing liberal with dangerously naïve foreign policy views." Nixon added, "If you were running for the House or Senate, it would do. But you are running for President." Bush appreciated the advice, said he would take it, but ultimately would side with Atwater, fearing the consequences of a sustained slide in the polls. "Please keep sending me those Nixonian tidbits," Bush wrote to the former president on June 4, in a quick, personalized note, the kind that he loved to send to friends and potential supporters. "We are going to ratchet up spelling the differences with Dukakis as soon as the California primary is over; but I will take your advice and not go the 'hatchet' route. Incidentally Gov. John Sununu is proving very effective in debunking the 'miracle' of Massachusetts."

In his victory speech after winning the California primary on June 7, Bush launched an attack on Dukakis's patriotism. "I do not question the family values of Michael Dukakis, I don't question the love of his family one for the other." But, he added, "I'll never understand, when it came to his desk, why he vetoed a bill that called for the Pledge of Allegiance to be said in the schools of Massachusetts. I'll never understand it. We are one nation under God. Our kids should say the Pledge of Allegiance." A few days later he attacked Dukakis for having endorsed a state program that allowed convicted murderers to leave prisons for weekend furloughs. "Let 'em stay where they belong," cried Bush.

Bush's efforts to paint Dukakis into a liberal corner were beginning to work, when the Massachusetts governor outmaneuvered him. Just as John Connally and Texas conservative Democrats had done in 1970, Michael Dukakis enlisted Lloyd Bentsen to defeat George Bush. The selection of the smooth-talking conservative Texas senator as his running mate translated into an even larger lead over Bush in the polls. Following the Democratic convention in Atlanta, Bush trailed by seventeen percentage points, the widest gap so far in the race.

Bush had been thinking about choosing a running mate since he beat back Dole's surge in New Hampshire. Dole was among those considered. So, too, was Congressman Jack Kemp, a former Buffalo Bills quarterback and a leading conservative. The way Bush ultimately arrived at this decision would say much about his leadership style. He made the decision alone without a family conference or a meeting of his inner circle of advisers: James Baker, Lee Atwater, Robert Teeter, and Roger Ailes. He had been keeping an eye on a young senator from Indiana, Dan Quayle, who in some ways reminded Bush of himself at an earlier age. Quayle was the scion of a prominent family of newspaper publishers and had made a name for himself as a young man. In 1980 he had taken on an incumbent senator and won, knocking off the liberal icon Birch Bayh. Quayle was more ideologically conservative than Bush and had established links to the evangelical movement. Despite these advantages, Bush's advisers did not consider him a prime candidate for the post. The man who counted, however, did. At some point just before the Republican convention in New Orleans, Bush saw Quayle on one of the Sunday newsmaker television programs, where he had defended the Reagan-Bush record very well.

The first person that Bush told of his choice was his wife, Barbara. She learned on the plane to New Orleans. When they landed, Bush told President Reagan, who was leaving the city after his farewell to the convention the night before. James Baker heard when Ronald Reagan did, and, for him, it was an unwelcome surprise. Not only was Quayle insufficiently known to the Bush campaign, but Baker knew of better candidates. But the choice was Bush's, and it was made. Bush wanted to announce his selection at Spanish Square, where he was already scheduled to appear after a ninety-minute steamboat river cruise down the Mississippi. At 2:00 P.M., just before boarding the boat, Bush called Quayle to give him the news.

The result was mayhem. Quayle, who knew that he was on a short list of candidates, had been expecting some kind of call. What he and his wife, Marilyn, were not ready for was their introduction to a national audience ninety minutes hence. Because

George Bush wanted the secret to keep until the official announcement, there was no advance work to ensure that the Quayles made it to the square on time. As the Bushes steamed down the Mississippi, the square filled to overflowing with reveling conventioneers. The Quayles had to push through the crowd on their own, and a catastrophe was averted only because the Secret Service parted the crowd like the Red Sea. But with adrenaline pumping, Quayle failed his first test as a national figure. He leaped onto the stage like a teenager and proceeded to hug George Bush and punch him playfully in the arm. The situation soon got worse. There was another critical difference between Quayle and the young Bush. Quayle had not served his country in combat when men his age were in Vietnam. Immediately the Bush campaign entered crisis mode to determine if Quayle had been a draft dodger or had simply found a convenient way to avoid going overseas by joining the National Guard. The latter proved to be the case, but Quayle's awkwardness in answering questions about that period of his life and the Bush team's apparent surprise at this problem introduced a new vulnerability into the campaign.

The bungling of the choice of a running mate placed even more pressure on Bush to give a strong acceptance speech at the convention. Never good at prepared speeches, Bush brought in Ronald Reagan's most famous wordsmith, Peggy Noonan, to help. "He speaks in gusts," Noonan later recalled of her challenge with Bush. Most of the speech was drafted without controversy. But it lacked a punch line. Bush, himself, could not give Noonan anything other than a string of adjectives and sentence fragments: "Everyone matters . . . the handicapped . . . the kid in that Harlem (????) hospital 'thrown away' by Drug addicted AIDS ridden parents—Good God we must help that child." Noonan suggested a one-line reaffirmation of the antitax pledge that Bush started making in New Hampshire. She and campaign communications adviser Roger Ailes wanted something that sounded tough. Inspired by the toughness of Clint

Eastwood's "Make my day" catchphrase in the Dirty Harry movies, they came up with "Read my lips: No new taxes." (Eastwood, who was then also serving as the Republican mayor of Carmel, California, had been briefly considered as a running mate.)

The pragmatists around Bush hated the line. Richard Darman, a sometime economics adviser and protégé of James Baker, believed that taxes were inevitably going to have to play a role in solving the deficit problem. He argued against the phrase, knowing that Bush would eventually have to break it. But he was overruled. Bush had campaigned on this pledge, he had knitted together a coalition of his own in the party because of it, and it was time to share it with a national audience.

Remarkably, despite the internal turmoil in the campaign over the choice of Quayle, Bush's convention speech of absolutes coupled with the appeal of Reagan nostalgia allowed Bush to close the gap with Dukakis. In September Bush pulled ahead in the polls by attacking Dukakis for being weak on defense and then, in a spark of mischievous creativity, for being less of an environmentalist than he. In September he went to Boston Harbor to pledge more active environmental measures as president than Dukakis had offered in Massachusetts as governor.

And then there was Willie Horton. The campaign ad that would come to define the negativity of the 1988 campaign was produced by an independent group, "Americans for Bush," and—according to the Bush biographer Herbert S. Parmet—aired over twenty-eight days starting in mid-September. In attacking Dukakis for not being sufficiently tough on crime, the ad told the story of Willie Horton, a convicted murderer who slashed a man and raped his wife while on a weekend furlough sanctioned by the Massachusetts prison system. Although many other states had furlough programs, Massachusetts was alone in offering this program to first-degree murderers. Dukakis's support for this program had first been criticized by Al Gore during the Democratic primary, and Bush had started attacking Dukakis for the program in June, citing the Horton case, but it was the pro-Bush ad that drew national attention to the issue. It also caused a firestorm of criticism of Bush's supporters for appealing to racism because Horton was an African American. This, in turn, resulted in television news organizations repeating the ad around the country. Meanwhile the Bush campaign aired its own attack ad on the furlough program that raised the Horton case more subtly. Millions saw the darkened images of prisoners entering a turnstile. Although the official Bush campaign spot did not show any images of Horton, the media linked the two ads and aired the convict's mug shot. So, too, did flyers sent out by state Republican organizations. Letting the press magnify your fear advertising for you was an old political trick developed by Lyndon Johnson with his "daisy ad" in 1964 and refined by Charles Colson for Richard Nixon. And it worked for George Bush in 1988.

Despite these attacks and Dukakis's own campaign errors (for instance, letting himself be filmed in a tank, looking goofy in an ill-fitting helmet), the Massachusetts governor remained within striking distance. The first presidential debate in October drew little blood. And Bentsen did well in his only debate with Quayle, scoring with the instantly classic rebuff when Quayle compared his qualifications to those of John F. Kennedy in 1960. "I served with Jack Kennedy," Bentsen retorted in a line that he had prepared. (Quayle had been making this comparison on the campaign trail.) "I knew Jack Kennedy. Jack Kennedy was a friend of mine. Senator, you're no Jack Kennedy." But Dukakis sealed his own fate in the second debate. When asked whether he would rethink his own opposition to the death penalty if his wife, Kitty, were ever raped and killed, Dukakis responded impassively as if this were a question on the bar examination. His numbers plummeted, and he never recovered.

On November 8, 1988, Bush won forty states and 53 percent of the popular vote. Equally impressive was the number of no-shows at the polls. Only 50 percent of eligible American voters bothered to participate, the lowest turnout rate since World War II. Most political observers of the 1988 presidential campaign, and many voters, had found it not only uninspiring and overly negative but worrisome. The only mandate it produced, wrote Garry Wills in *Time*, was to "ignore the threats to our economy, sustain the Reagan heritage of let's pretend, and serve as a figurehead for what America has become, a frightened empire hiding its problems from itself."

Declines in the stock market and in the U.S. dollar in overseas markets that followed the election left Bush little time to savor the victory. Questions arose as to how he would manage the budget deficit. On November 17 the chairman of the Federal Reserve, Alan Greenspan, testified before the National Economic Commission that cutting the federal budget deficit was "becoming ever more urgent. How it is done is far less relevant than that it be done." Less than a week later, former presidents Gerald Ford and Jimmy Carter added their voices, suggesting that tax increases would inevitably be part of the solution. Publicly and privately, they advised the president-elect to "face reality" and drop his "no new taxes" pledge.

Bush resisted. In his first press conference after his election victory, he reiterated the pledge and even promised to press for reductions in capital gains taxes. It is not clear that Bush believed that the combination of the flexible freeze and further tax cuts would work, but he knew that he had no choice. There was one Republican elder statesman who seemed to agree. After the Congressional Budget Office revised upward its forecast for the deficit in 1990, Richard Nixon sent a fax to George Bush and "six mutual friends." Nixon urged that Bush hang tough in the face of these pressures. In response, Bush typed a note himself dated December 16, 1988, that expressed his gratitude. "I agree with it. To roll over on the Read My Lips pleadge [*sic*] would guarantee oblivion."

On the eve of attaining the presidency, a prize he had pursued for years, George Bush faced a daunting domestic challenge made worse by the manner he had employed to get this prize. Over the course of his career as a presidential appointee and then as vice president, Bush had already come to prefer dealing with foreign policy. Now, as he prepared for his inauguration, the president-elect understood that it would not be enough just to hope for more workable challenges abroad.

3

Cleaning Up Reagan's Mess

America is never wholly herself unless she is engaged
in high moral principle. We as a people have such a
purpose today. It is to make kinder the face of the
Nation and gentler the face of the world.

—George H. W. Bush, January 20, 1989

Ronald Reagan was a hard act to follow. As the first man elected
to succeed a president of the same party since Herbert Hoover
moved into the White House in 1929, George Bush faced the immediate challenge of defining his presidency. Hoover, at least, had
started out with a positive reputation that was distinct from that
of his predecessor, Calvin Coolidge. Yet the election campaign of
1988, so long on patriotic symbols and so short on substance, had
left only a vague impression of the incoming president, certainly
nothing as powerful as the public image of Ronald Reagan, who
despite Iran-Contra appeared to be departing directly from 1600
Pennsylvania Avenue for Mount Rushmore. The mantra within the
Bush camp was that this friendly takeover had to be understood as
Bush I and not Reagan III. Although the concern was real, the case
that this would be a different government turned out to be not
that hard to make. More than stylistic differences separated these
two chief executives. The media would focus on Bush's vow of a

"kinder" nation, first made at the convention in New Orleans and later in his inaugural address, as symbolic of his rejection of the frontier-style capitalism associated with Reagan. And indeed, Bush would soon show in his domestic policy that he had a less pinched view than Reagan of the proper role of government in American society. But in the context of the times it was the incoming president's suspicion of Reagan's late-term embrace of Mikhail Gorbachev that represented the most dramatic departure. George Bush entered the White House unsure whether the Cold War was actually coming to an end.

Bush's first appointment, announced a few days after the election, provided no hint of what was to come. Bush named James Baker, his longtime confidant from Houston, as secretary of state. Baker, who had been Reagan's first chief of staff and later his secretary of the Treasury, was an exquisitely groomed lawyer and political operative out of central casting, whose script could have been the billionaire-celebrity Donald Trump's bestselling book, *The Art of the Deal*. Although smart and savvy, the secretary of state–designate was not known for having any overarching foreign policy views. But in Bush's choice of Brent Scowcroft as national security adviser, the president-elect signaled a return to the realist foreign policies of the Nixon and Ford years. In sum, a realist foreign policy is grounded in the actual interests of the United States—economic, military, political—and the actual international balance of power and is less susceptible to ideological crusades or romanticism. Reagan's dream of a nuclear-free world, for example, had been a problem for realists because they suspected it had driven him to compromise with Gorbachev. Scowcroft had served as Henry Kissinger's deputy from 1973 to 1975, after which he succeeded Kissinger as national security adviser when Gerald Ford decided Kissinger should be satisfied with just being secretary of state. The hardworking former air force general had been a student of the influential realist scholar Hans Morgenthau and brought an exceptionally sharp mind to the task of discerning U.S. national interests. Scowcroft viewed the Reagan administration's handling of U.S.-Soviet relations with increasing alarm. Like many of the realists of his generation, he believed that the Soviets had exploited the spirit of détente in the late 1970s to make gains against the United States, and he feared Gorbachev was playing the same game. He shared George Bush's concern about the INF Treaty, which came into force in June 1988 and eliminated all nuclear-armed intermediate-range (300–3,400 miles) ballistic and cruise missiles. Indeed, what mattered to Scowcroft were the facts on the ground: the number of Soviet nuclear warheads pointed at the United States, the number of Soviet tanks in eastern Europe, and the amount of Soviet assistance to its third world allies. In these areas the Kremlin's actions still did not fully match Gorbachev's rhetoric. Moreover, whatever one thought about Gorbachev as an individual, he was just one man. Were Gorbachev to be replaced (as was Nikita Khrushchev in 1964), Scowcroft believed that his legacy could be wiped out quickly by a new hard-line leadership. Scowcroft did not want the United States to disarm prematurely— materially or psychologically—and had made his criticisms of the previous administration's management of foreign affairs most strikingly as one of the authors of the Tower Commission report on Iran-Contra. A week or so after Scowcroft's nomination, Henry Kissinger himself weighed in with a supportive op-ed article in the *Washington Post* timed to coincide with Gorbachev's final summit with Reagan. Critical of the approach taken by Reagan and Secretary of State George Shultz, Kissinger suggested that the new Bush team would bring a welcome wariness to the relationship with the Soviet leader.

When the summit occurred on December 7, 1988, Bush accompanied President Reagan and Secretary Shultz to meet with Gorbachev at Governors Island in New York Harbor. Opting not to bring Baker or Scowcroft along, Bush chose instead to act as vice president and not as president-elect. Bush smiled and said little, melting into the patriotic background with the Statue of Liberty visible across the harbor. Over lunch, Bush hinted at skepticism about the future of Gorbachev's reforms. And when he asked the Soviet leader what U.S. investors could expect from perestroika in three to five years, Gorbachev answered, "Even Jesus Christ couldn't answer that question." Bush's demeanor managed to both annoy Shultz—who would later heap scorn on Bush's performance—and worry Gorbachev, who left New York wondering whether Bush was a closet hawk.

Gorbachev had a right to expect more from his new partner. The Governors Island meeting came on the heels of the most important speech ever given by a Soviet leader at the United Nations. Earlier in the day Gorbachev had announced the unilateral withdrawal of thousands of Soviet troops from eastern Europe. Though in the past Nikita Khrushchev and Leonid Brezhnev had announced unilateral troop cutbacks, what made this announcement historic was that Gorbachev admitted that these Warsaw Pact forces had been operating under an offensive strategy that would now end. And by wrapping the announcement of the withdrawal of Soviet forces from eastern Europe in rhetoric about national self-determination, Gorbachev was also hinting at an end to the Soviet policy of using force to prevent change in eastern Europe.

Bush's goal at Governors Island had not been to seem impolite. In a pattern that would be repeated often in the administration to come, he was prepared to risk the appearance of apathy as the wheels turned in his mind as to what his next step should be. Among intimates these were the periods of the "listening Bush." Bush had seen the changes in eastern Europe with his own eyes. In 1987 he had visited Poland, where he had met both the Polish Communist leader Wojciech Jaruzelski and the leader of the opposition Solidarity movement, Lech Walesa. But, as yet, he had not concluded how best to use the relationship with Gorbachev to help Walesa and the other new democrats achieve their goals. In a little-noticed gesture, Bush showed at the time of the Governors Island meeting that he knew he would have to build a working relationship with the Soviet leadership. Just after giving his speech, Gorbachev had received word of a devastating earthquake near Yerevan, the capital of the Soviet republic of Armenia. Bush's personal touch was to send his son Jeb and his twelve-year-old grandson George P. to that Soviet republic to show his concern and to give him a firsthand report on the tragedy.

· · ·

George Bush's inaugural address six weeks later was more articulate and stirring than many had expected. In marked distinction from his predecessor, he made an appeal for public service, though in offering the metaphor "a thousand points of light" he emphasized voluntary activism and charitable organizations more than joining the government. On the Cold War, however, Bush echoed some of Reagan's optimism for the meaning of recent events. "The totalitarian era is passing," he celebrated, with a simile that would have confounded an arborist, "its old ideas blown away like leaves from an ancient, lifeless tree." Yet in his first actions the new president continued to show caution toward Gorbachev and the Soviet Union, suspending all substantive U.S.-Soviet contacts until the completion of a strategic review of American policy toward Moscow and the Soviet bloc.

As the strategic review started, Bush found himself in a bruising struggle with the Congress over his choice for secretary of defense. Bush wanted his longtime ally former senator John Tower of Texas in the job. As chairman of the Senate Armed Services Committee in the early 1980s, Tower had been a forceful proponent of defense spending but had not shied away from criticizing inefficiency at the Pentagon. And, as the chairman of the Tower Commission set up to investigate the Iran-Contra scandal, he had handled another difficult task effectively. Senators traditionally confirm their former colleagues with ease, but Tower had made many powerful enemies, most notably Senator Sam Nunn, Democrat of Georgia and the incumbent chairman of the Armed Services Committee. These enemies sank the nomination by allowing gossip about Tower's womanizing and drinking to so cloud the matter that he became the first cabinet nominee of an incoming president to lose a confirmation vote. As Tower's replacement, Bush chose Representative Dick Cheney of Wyoming, the House minority whip, who had been Gerald Ford's chief of staff in the mid-1970s.

One area of foreign policy where the incoming administration knew its mind and showed some leadership was in Central America. Bush moved quickly to manage the two very difficult problems that he had inherited there. In March 1989 the Congress would face a vote on supplying the Contras. Bush and Baker understood two things about the Nicaraguan problem. First, there was no more divisive foreign policy issue. Members of Congress and their staffs had spent most of the 1980s disputing how and whether the United States should seek the overthrow of the Sandinista government of Daniel Ortega. Second, the new Bush administration lacked the votes in Congress to pass any military assistance package for the Contras. Not wanting his first foreign policy initiative to result in a humiliating personal defeat, Bush chose to make Nicaraguan policy a showcase for a new bipartisanship in Washington. Over the objection of the hard Right, he chose a Democrat, Bernard Aronson, as assistant secretary of state for inter-American affairs. Building upon an agreement that the Central American presidents had made for themselves in 1987, under the leadership of Oscar Arias of Costa Rica, the administration then approached the Democrats with a plan to provide humanitarian support to the Contras while applying pressure on the Sandinistas to support full and free elections in February 1990. Following a month of intensive negotiations, Senate majority leader George Mitchell of Maine accepted the plan in March 1989, announcing that he "trusted" the intentions of the new president and secretary of state. The administration would drop military efforts to overthrow Ortega's government and vowed to accept the results of a free election. Meanwhile Congress would provide $50 million in humanitarian assistance to the Contras through February 1990 but had the option to review the policy in November. The Contra half of the Iran-Contra political scandal—which had nearly destroyed one presidency and threatened a second—had disappeared. In February 1990 Violetta Barrios de Chamorro would be elected president over Daniel Ortega. So, too, did the Iranian side of the scandal disappear. Quietly, George Bush stopped talking about the hostages being held by Iranian-backed Hezbollah in Beirut; the new team looked to intelligence and covert action to find and free them.

A second problem in Central America seemed much less susceptible to a political solution. The Reagan administration's negotiations with the Panamanian dictator Manuel Noriega had produced nothing but an internal fight with Vice President Bush and criticism for hypocrisy from those who recalled Reagan's tough rhetoric on drug dealers. Despite an offer to drop the two Miami indictments against him for drug dealing, Noriega had refused to leave office. Bush authorized a resumption of talks with Noriega in early 1989 but emphasized that under no circumstances would his administration renew the offer to drop the indictments. In response, Noriega staged a corrupt and bloody election in May that underscored his unwillingness to leave office, as his supporters roughed up opposition leaders and international observers noted widespread voter fraud. The Bush administration stepped up efforts to encourage a coup against Noriega by the Panamanian Defense Force and replaced the commander of the U.S. Southern Command, which would have responsibility for any military action in Panama. Unlike his predecessor, the new commander, General Maxwell Thurman, was prepared to use force to remove Noriega if all other approaches failed. In October the wife of a member of Noriega's personal security guard approached the United States with a request for assistance. The coup plotters wanted the U.S. Army to block two routes to prevent

Noriega from reinforcing his positions in Panama City in the event of a coup. Skeptical about the coup's leader and surprisingly ill-prepared to handle a military crisis, the administration fumbled its response when the coup was attempted on October 3, 1989. Belatedly, U.S. forces did block the two routes, but Noriega's allies used a commercial airport to fly in reinforcements to rescue Noriega, who was being detained in his presidential palace by the coup plotters. Within a matter of hours, Noriega was back in power, the leaders of the coup were dead, and the United States looked impotent.

• • •

In his inaugural address, Bush vowed to bring the federal budget into balance, and though he understood that government had a role to play in society, the deficits meant that the country had "more will than wallet." As he strove to clean up Reagan's messes in Latin America and the Middle East, Bush also turned to some inescapable problems at home.

The White House and Congress had little control over most of the federal budget in 1989. More than 65 percent of the budget comprised mandatory spending programs and so-called entitlements (Medicaid, Medicare, Social Security, veterans benefits, food stamps, and school lunch programs), which were very popular and effectively could not be reduced. Of the remaining 35 percent, defense took a large chunk, leaving very little for Congress or the president to play with. Since 1974, Congress prevented presidents from deciding not to spend money that been appropriated using something called *impoundment*. Presidents since Richard Nixon had therefore fought for the ability to strike out particular items in the budget passed and sent to them by Congress. Understandably, Congress never had an interest in granting this line-item veto. On the revenue side, Ronald Reagan had convinced Americans that they could have their entitlements, which since the inflation-ridden 1970s were indexed to inflation, and their tax giveaways, such as mortgage-interest deductions, and still pay less in personal income taxes. As George Bush and the moderates around him understood, the math could not work. Nevertheless, reluctant to break his "no new taxes" pledge, Bush wanted to try the flexible freeze approach. Although many economists were arguing that the budget deficit was itself a drag on the economy—because of the higher interest rates that it produced—Bush hoped for enough economic growth to bring a significant increase in tax revenues.

As difficult budgetary decisions loomed, Bush also found himself confronted with an expanding crisis among financial institutions called "savings and loans," or thrifts. The savings and loan crisis was the product of bad policy and greed. In the 1930s Congress had regulated the thrift industry to ensure a pool of capital for the U.S. housing market. Thrifts, which were restricted to investing deposits in thirty-year mortgages, were to make money on the difference between short-term rates on deposit accounts and higher long-term mortgage rates. The system worked fine until the stagflation of the 1970s, when both inflation and interest rates went up. Because of the caps on the rates they could offer depositors, thrifts were losing deposits to money market accounts offered by investment houses. By 1980 almost all of the country's 4,000 savings and loan associations were insolvent. In response, Congress made the situation worse by allowing the thrifts to offer higher interest rates and reducing the amount of money that they had to keep in reserve. Congress also increased the amount in a single deposit account that was federally insured from $40,000 to $100,000. Within two years, the value of the reserves of the S&Ls plummeted from $31 billion to $4 billion, as the thrifts found themselves paying 18 percent on deposit accounts while receiving just 8 percent in return from established mortgages. With estimates of $100 billion to clean up the mess and refund all of the depositors, Congress responded to the pleas for help from the thrifts by another round of deregulation. Culminating in the Garn-St. Germain

Depository Institutions Act of 1982, Congress permitted S&Ls to act even more like banks, allowing investment in business and commercial real estate in search of a better return. Ronald Reagan called it the "most important legislation for financial institutions in the last fifty years," but in practice the act unleashed a wave of corruption, theft, and mismanagement. As the analysts Robert E. Litan and Jonathan Rauch concluded for the Brookings Institution in 1998, the fall in interest rates by the mid-1980s had already lowered the cost of fixing the thrift system to $15 billion because most S&Ls were headed for solvency. But the deregulation of the early 1980s thrust a once heavily regulated industry into a totally unfamiliar investment environment. Over the next four years S&Ls in Texas and California tripled in size as these institutions took the lead in the real estate boom in the West and Southwest. By 1985 S&Ls were again failing at an alarming rate. In the states of Ohio and Maryland these failures depleted state insurance funds. By 1987 the crisis had hit Texas, where dramatic S&L failures caused a statewide recession as housing values plummeted and lending dried up.

If the problem had not caught Bush's attention before, it did when the Texas economy plummeted in 1987 and his son Neil was pulled into the widening vortex of trouble because of his position on the board of the Silverado Savings and Loan, which issued bad loans to people who were investing in the younger Bush's oil exploration company. In 1986 and 1987 Congress pumped $15 billion and then $10.7 billion into the Federal Savings and Loan Insurance Corporation. Although the issue did not figure in the 1988 campaign, the FSLIC fell even farther into the red as more S&Ls defaulted and depositors wanted to get their money back.

George Bush had not been without responsibility for this mess. As vice president he had served on a commission that had argued for more deregulation of the U.S. economy and made no exception for the S&L industry. On a smaller scale, Bush had watched as his friends and campaign contributors put money into Silverado. So, on December 30, 1988, as president-elect, Bush asked Richard Darman, the incoming director of the Office of Management and Budget, to give him a seminar on the S&L problem and what the U.S. government could do about it.

Bush already understood that he had to move fast to do something about the S&L crisis. Darman confirmed for the president that the problem could not wait, and argued that though the cost to U.S. taxpayers would be high, if insolvent thrifts were not closed soon the cost would get even bigger. Bush agreed and decided to push for congressional action. In August 1989 Congress abolished the FSLIC and provided the Federal Deposit Insurance Corporation with $50 billion in lending authority to deal with the problem. What all of this meant was that the federal government would allow more S&Ls to collapse and try to help depositors through insurance payments. As expected, the short-term effects were foreclosures across the country, especially in the Southwest, and a severe downturn in the national housing market. Ultimately the cleanup would cost $161 billion, of which $132 billion came from public funds.

The S&L cleanup placed an unwanted, but necessary, burden on the federal budget. In discussions with his advisers in the early weeks of the administration, Bush explained that he would not permit taxes as a remedy for at least the first year of his term. He wanted everything other than increasing taxes to be tried before he broke his most important electoral promise. Instead, Bush wanted to engage in negotiations with the Democrats over the 1990 budget, which would serve as the first phase in reining in expenditures. Unfortunately for the new president, he was unable to control his own advisers. An effort to force the Pentagon to accept a freeze on the growth in the defense budget failed. Against the unified opposition of his secretary of defense, Dick Cheney, the Joint Chiefs of Staff, and Brent Scowcroft, Bush agreed to only a one-year freeze followed by 1 percent increases each of the next two years and a 2 percent increase at the end of his term. Combined with Bush's campaign promises to increase spending on the environment and on education, this meant that the budget deficit would grow worse unless the economy grew at an unexpectedly large rate.

Conservatives argued that the only way to get the growth needed to solve the budget problem was to cut capital gains taxes. Historically capital gains had been taxed at a lower rate than ordinary income, but since the tax reform of 1986 all types of income had been treated the same and now capital gains were subject to the same top rate of 28 percent as wages and salaries. Some economists argued that as a result of the increase in capital gains taxes, Americans held on to investments longer and made fewer investments. Bush agreed and had promised to cut these taxes. Democratic leaders, especially Majority Leader Mitchell, strenuously argued that at a time when the country needed to show fiscal discipline it made no sense, and sent the wrong signal, to give a tax break to stockholders. Mitchell explained that in return for his willingness to participate in budget negotiations in 1989, the White House had to agree not to raise capital gains tax reductions that year. Forced to choose between congressional Republicans who were eager to force the issue and Mitchell and the Democrats, Bush decided to make a futile push for capital gains tax reductions, causing only anger among his Democratic negotiating partners. The budget was one Reagan mess that Bush did not clean up in his first year.

•   •   •

Remarkably, given the new administration's relative activism and creativity on other fronts, Bush and Scowcroft let the U.S.-Soviet policy review continue for months, stalling the progress that the Reagan administration had made in transforming the relationship with Gorbachev. Indeed, this was one area where Reagan had not left a mess for Bush to clean up. In the words of James Baker, what followed was "neither truly strategic, nor a proper review." And the result, again according to Baker, was "mush." The problem was not so much that this review was conducted by so many Reagan holdovers who disliked it—the excuse later given by the Bush administration—but that the new Bush team could not agree on a strategy. There was an irony to this. In contrast with previous administrations, Bush's three principal national security officials—the secretary of state, the national security adviser, and the secretary of defense—had all worked together with the president in a previous administration (under Gerald Ford), and all still got along. Yet despite the good feeling and mutual respect, these men often disagreed on matters of substance. Baker and Cheney defined the two extremes in the advice that Bush received on Gorbachev. Baker sought maximum tactical flexibility to work with the Soviet leader, whereas Cheney assumed that Gorbachev would fail, wanted to let him fail, and hoped to take advantage of Soviet weakness. Scowcroft was always somewhere in the middle, leaving President Bush holding the balance of power. What made the system work was that once Bush decided, the policy was loyally followed. Bush's instinct in the first months was to take no decisive action and watch Gorbachev a little longer.

The Bush team's disagreements and the president's uncertainty accurately reflected the debate going on among the experts within the broader U.S. national security community. There were three main questions. One was whether Gorbachev's objective was a strategic respite to allow the Soviets to compete more effectively for international influence, as seemed to have been their goal in the 1970s; or, second, whether Gorbachev was a true reformer who was prepared to change the nature of the Soviet empire, even at the cost of Soviet control of the satellites. The third question followed

from the second: if Gorbachev was a real reformer, could he succeed without falling victim to a putsch led by the hard-liners?

Had U.S. intelligence been able to peer inside the Kremlin,
Washington would have seen that the reformers in Gorbachev's
inner circle also wondered about the direction he was taking. "The
contradiction between our general policy on foreign affairs and the
ongoing practice of Soviet arms exports is becoming ever more
striking," wrote his key national security aide, Anatoly Chernyaev,
in September 1988. "On the one hand, we are increasingly striving
for the realization of a reduction in conventional arms. On the
other hand, every week, or even several times a week, the Central
Committee gets proposals to fulfill the armament needs of various
friendly and not-so-friendly countries . . . Our almost unfailing
readiness to comply with those requests (sometimes even demands) not only harms our relations with the West but also hurts
the prospects of our peace offensive." The habits of empire, even
for the most dedicated reformer, were hard to break. But the reformers in Moscow knew that Gorbachev was for real. In Washington, where old habits were equally resilient, the contradictions
between Gorbachev's welcome rhetoric and his government's action gave ammunition to the cautious and the hawkish alike. The
intelligence community and the Pentagon were honeycombed with
skeptics who welcomed what they interpreted as the return to realism under the Bush team.

The pause in managing Gorbachev created a bad first impression
about Bush's abilities as president. It seemed remarkable that someone who had served as an understudy for the job for eight years
needed this much time to make up his mind about the most important issue in international affairs, an area that by all accounts he
considered his strong suit. Yet Bush was not idle. He was working
behind the scenes to gather information and establish high-level
friendships as his advisers argued about Gorbachev and he thought

through what to do. Sensing that relations with France would be very important as events unfolded in Europe, Bush made a point of reaching out to French president François Mitterrand. Mitterrand and Reagan had thoroughly disliked each other, and so the invitation to visit the Bush compound at the Maine resort of Kennebunkport came as a surprise to the Elysée Palace, but the visit in May 1989 was a grand success. Although he believed that British prime minister Margaret Thatcher had been much too quick to declare the Cold War over (she had made that statement in 1988), Bush listened to his European allies, and they, in turn, tried to convince Gorbachev that eventually Bush would come around. West German chancellor Helmut Kohl even pointed out to Gorbachev that unlike Nancy Reagan, the new first lady Barbara Bush "is a steady, balanced woman, [who] has a calming effect on people."

As the U.S. government debated with itself, the unraveling of the Soviet empire in Europe began to accelerate. Poland was the scene of the first dramatic change. In February 1989 Solidarity was legalized and Walesa entered into talks with the Communist government to prepare for a new electoral system. In June Solidarity won every contested seat in the Polish lower house (by agreement the Communists were assigned 65 percent of the seats) and all but one seat in the Polish Senate. Seeing himself also as a great nationalist, the Communist leader Wojciech Jaruzelski responded to the defeat by agreeing to share power. In Hungary a group of reform Communists, whom Gorbachev approvingly considered miniature versions of himself, opened the border to Austria in May 1989 and then watched as East Germans tried to use this opening in the Iron Curtain to escape their own country.

These events prompted Bush to reveal more of his private passion for the democrats in eastern Europe. Traditionally, since Yugoslavia split from Stalin in 1948, the United States had supported regimes that were thorns in Moscow's side. Bush mandated that henceforth eastern European regimes were to be rewarded for liberalizing and for supporting Gorbachev. The promise came in a speech to a Polish-American group in Michigan in April 1989; but the move did little to dispel the image of a passive administration. "Rewarding" these regimes was not to involve cash. Worried about the already ballooning federal deficit, the White House chose not to make any dramatic grants, just promising to support Polish requests for international loans. Bush himself shared the caution of his Treasury secretary, Nicholas Brady, an old Wall Street hand, who worried that lacking any real fiscal plan these governments would send the money to private accounts in Switzerland.

While Bush moved ever so slightly to help the reform movement in Poland, the realism of his administration's foreign policy faced an unexpected test outside Europe. The wave of democratization had reached the shores of China. On a visit to China in mid-May, Mikhail Gorbachev was greeted in Beijing's Tiananmen Square by hundreds of thousands of friendly demonstrators, mainly young students, who had started taking to the streets and calling for a Chinese perestroika since the death of Hu Yaobang, the former general secretary of the Chinese Communist Party and a fellow reformer, in April. The scene was so chaotic that Gorbachev mentioned to his own entourage, "Who the hell is in charge here?" When the students refused to leave the square following Gorbachev's visit and erected a makeshift statue of liberty, a tense standoff began. The Chinese leadership panicked, especially after a first attempt to use armed units from Beijing to clear the square failed when some of the troops began fraternizing with the students. On June 4 the leadership ordered units from the provinces to open fire to scatter the demonstrators. An estimated 3,000 died and 10,000 were injured in the melee that followed. For much of the world, which watched in horror, the meaning of the event was captured by the image of a lone Chinese protester attempting to stare down a line of tanks.

For days the Chinese leadership refused to speak to any Western leader, including George Bush, though he was the one non-Communist leader whom the Chinese knew best. As the tension mounted in the square, Bush had attempted to telephone to plead for restraint, but none of his calls was taken. Then he started sending letters to Deng Xiaoping, the recently retired leader whom Bush had first met over fifteen years earlier when he was the U.S. representative in the Chinese capital. With official silence as the Chinese response to the world's outrage at the mass murder, Bush faced the question of what to do about the U.S. government's nearly twenty-year policy of engagement. With demands for freedom stirring around the world, was this not the time to send a tough signal to authoritarian governments? What lesson might the Soviets or the East Germans, for example, take from a successful crackdown in Beijing? These were difficult questions, especially because Bush was convinced that the Chinese were so xenophobic they would not take criticism well. Finally, convinced of the strategic importance of the U.S. relationship with China, Bush resolved that he needed to try to rebuild it at whatever political cost. "We must walk our way through this," Bush told his advisers.

"I write this letter to you with a heavy heart," Bush wrote to Deng on June 20. Bush asked for clemency for the student demonstrators and appealed to Deng to do what he could to preserve the Sino-American relationship. Publicly the administration had criticized the Chinese and cut all military-to-military ties between the two countries. But Bush was under pressure to do more, and he asked Deng to accept a personal emissary so that Bush could explain why he felt these measures necessary as well as his decision to protect a prominent Chinese dissident, Fang Lizhi, who had fled to the U.S. embassy. A day later Deng replied that he would welcome an official U.S. visitor. Bush then dispatched Brent Scowcroft on a secret mission to let the Chinese know that though the United States was disappointed in their handling of the student protests, and believed domestic reforms were inevitable, the relationship had to continue. The Chinese captured Scowcroft on tape toasting their leadership and made sure the world saw it.

The events in China helped Bush make up his mind about what to do about Gorbachev. A month after the Tiananmen massacre, Bush went on a very public visit to Hungary and Poland to lend his personal support to the democratic developments there. Crowds turned out in the streets, and though he found Lech Walesa on this trip to be a "showboat," he was again deeply affected by the passion in the air and the energy and resolve of the reformers he met. Determined that they would not experience the fate of those in China, Bush did not even wait to return to the United States to send a personal note to Gorbachev. In a letter dated July 21 he proposed a face-to-face meeting "without thousands of assistants hovering over our shoulders, without the ever-present briefing papers and certainly without the press yelling at us every five minutes about 'who's winning,' 'what agreements have been reached,' or 'has our meeting succeeded or failed.'" Until that moment Bush had believed that unstructured summits were dangerous because they raised expectations unnecessarily. But the times required them, as he put it to Gorbachev, to "reduce the chances there could be any misunderstandings between us" and to "get our relationship on a more personal basis." Now convinced that only engagement with the Soviet Union would solve the remaining questions about Soviet reform, Bush overturned the four-decade policy of containing the Soviet Union. Henceforth the United States would work to bring the Soviet Union more tightly into the international system. In return for the gains in terms of prestige and trade that would ensue, Moscow would be coaxed to accept new rules, above all the self-determination of all the states of east-central Europe and the reduction of military forces in that region.

Events would outpace the two leaders. After months of delay because of Bush's reluctance, now Gorbachev became the harder of the two leaders to schedule. He could meet in December 1989, at the earliest, in Malta. As it turned out, the two leaders were not going to be able to establish a personal connection before even more dramatic events would allow Gorbachev to prove to even the most stubborn cold warriors in Washington that he was for real.

4

Unexpected Greatness

As the Bush administration was still fumbling with its review of international affairs, Gorbachev once again set irrevocable changes in motion. This time it happened in East Germany, the most Stalinist redoubt of Moscow's European empire. Following the Soviet leader's attendance at a ceremony on October 7, 1989, to mark the fortieth anniversary of the German Democratic Republic, East Germans took to the streets to demand Gorbachevian reforms from their leader Erich Honecker, the man who had organized the building of the Berlin Wall in 1961. But when Honecker attempted to order his military to attack demonstrators in Leipzig days later, his colleagues refused to act like the Chinese. Instead they fired Honecker and attempted to mollify the crowds. But they continued to build into the hundreds of thousands, and after Gorbachev stated on October 25 that the Soviet Union did not believe it had the right to interfere in the domestic affairs of its allies, the regime lost any remaining control.

The last act of the nasty East German police state came in a moment of farce. At a press conference on November 9, designed to introduce new rules for travel to West Germany, the party chief in East Berlin, who was poorly briefed on the new system, mistakenly told reporters that free travel to the West would begin immediately. East Germans took him at his word and approached the Berlin controls. The police there, just as confused as the party chief, assumed it was all right to let them pass. That night thousands of Berliners jumped onto the Berlin Wall and, meeting no resistance from East German border guards, began to take sledgehammers to it. The twenty-eight-year-old wound dividing Berlin was no more.

At the end of the Cuban missile crisis in October 1962, John F. Kennedy warned his advisers that there should be no gloating about the victory over Soviet leader Nikita Khrushchev, whose bid to build a nuclear base in Cuba had failed. Similarly George Bush understood immediately that with the collapse of the Berlin Wall it was not in America's interests to rub salt in Moscow's wounds. The collapse of East Germany was a world historical defeat for the Kremlin. Since 1945 Moscow's armed presence deep in the heart of Hitler's former empire had been a major symbol of Soviet prestige. Three separate East-West crises over the status of Berlin followed (1948–49, 1958–59, 1961–63) until in the 1970s the United States and the Soviet Union formally recognized the division of the city and the division between the Germanies, which for a decade had been symbolized by a brutal wall. The seemingly accidental collapse of that symbol said much about what little was left of the once vaunted Soviet threat.

Bush wisely refused to show any exuberance for the cameras. When asked why he didn't "seem elated" at a hastily organized press conference on November 9, Bush answered carefully but dishonestly, "I am not an emotional kind of guy." That same month this extremely emotional man would ask his youngest son, Marvin, to read his eulogy for C. Fred Chambers at his dear friend's funeral service, because he knew he could not get through it without breaking down. But Bush chose to dissemble because this was not, as he told his advisers, the time "to dance on the wall." In fact, the listening Bush was gone, and an activist Bush took over.

George Bush had already been the most forward-leaning proponent of German reunification in the U.S. government. He knew the

German story as well as any of his advisers, having fought in World War II and watched the superpowers wrestle over the area in the decades since. He had been at the UN, after all, when Nixon's diplomacy and West German chancellor Willy Brandt's policy of *Ostpolitik* produced some normalization of the relations between East and West Germany. Now Bush sensed that there was a historic opportunity not only to reunify the country but to bring it into NATO and end the Cold War. He was confident that if he used his power wisely he might be able to help the Germans achieve what few had dared even dream of in their lifetime. He trusted the West German chancellor Helmut Kohl and, more important, believed the West Germans had developed into true democrats who had forsaken their parents' militarism. They had earned a chance at reunification and were needed in the Western alliance. Meanwhile Bush understood that he was getting way ahead of his allies, let alone Mikhail Gorbachev. Stunned by the political upheaval in Berlin, Gorbachev, Mitterrand, and Thatcher each told Bush that German unification, let alone a unified Germany in NATO, was not on the agenda. Referring to the lingering effects of the trauma of World War II, Thatcher advised Bush that "history here is living history." Gorbachev told an approving Mitterrand that if Germany reunified, a Soviet marshal would be in his seat in six months. Nevertheless, in the weeks and months that followed, the Bush administration would leave no doubt that it supported German self-determination while carefully leaving vague the sticky details of how or when this would happen. Equally important to Bush would be reassuring Moscow that it was witnessing a spontaneous, uncontrollable German movement that had no U.S. direction or involvement.

The long-planned and long-delayed summit at Malta followed a month after the collapse of the Berlin Wall. Here Bush would have a better opportunity to assess Gorbachev's reaction to the changes in Europe. Even he had started to complain that his administration's review was dragging on so long that the United States had effectively let Gorbachev take control of the international agenda. With the fall of the wall, no one could be said to be in control anymore, but at least Bush wanted to demonstrate to the Soviets and the world his government's recognition that a new international system was emerging. "Brief, brief, brief" was how Bush explained his preparation for the summit in a note to Richard Nixon, from whom he had asked for pointers. Confident of his approach, and feeling thirty years younger, Bush spent the evening before the meeting energetically walking around the USS *Belknap*, meeting its crew, and even taking time to fish off the guided missile cruiser's fantail.

The weather turned horrible the next day—the worst in decades, according to the Maltese—and what was supposed to be a two-day visit of choreographed shuttling between the U.S. cruiser and the Soviet ship became a superpower struggle against seasickness. The rolling waves confined the two leaders to a Soviet cruise liner, the *Maxim Gorky*, tied up at a pier. Despite these logistical problems, the summit was a turning point in the relationship between the two leaders. Although they had met before, Gorbachev and Bush took the measure of each other again and liked what they saw. During the first session, on December 2, Bush was candid about his approach to the unwinding events in eastern Europe. "There are people in the United States," he told Gorbachev in a statement that was also revealing about his own insecurities, "who accuse me of being too cautious. It is true I am a prudent man, but I am not a coward, and my administration will seek to avoid doing anything that would damage your position in the world. But I was insistently advised to do something of the sort—to climb the Berlin Wall and to make broad declarations. My administration, however, is avoiding these steps; we are in favor of reserved behavior." Bush's vow pleased Gorbachev. "I welcome your words," he said. "I regard them as a manifestation of political will. It is important for me."

No agreements were signed at Malta, but the two leaders agreed to sign a Conventional Forces in Europe (CFE) agreement by the end of 1990. Afterward Bush also instructed his advisers to prepare economic proposals that could be signed at the next summit with Gorbachev that would broaden the trading relationship between the two countries, establish an investment treaty, and grant Moscow observer status at the General Agreement on Tariffs and Trade (GATT) meetings.

Again events moved faster in eastern Europe than any leader had predicted. With the Kremlin clearly unwilling to intervene, popular uprisings toppled Communist dictatorships in Czechoslovakia and Bulgaria, and Nicolae Ceauşescu was overthrown in a bloody coup d'état in Romania. Meanwhile the East German regime appeared equally doomed.

The acceleration of world events had a liberating effect on Bush's characteristic caution. As dictatorships collapsed in Europe, Bush decided it was time to confront one closer to home. In the aftermath of the failed coup attempt in Panama, the president had ordered an acceleration of contingency planning. Stung by the reappearance of "wimp" criticism, Bush wanted to ensure that, should another opportunity arise to remove Manuel Noriega, his administration would not botch it. Noriega then gave Bush the pretext he wanted, announcing on December 15 that a state of war existed between the United States and Panama. The next day the Panamanian Defense Forces killed an unarmed U.S. marine after roughing up a U.S. Army lieutenant and his wife. When Bush heard of the death and that the lieutenant's wife had been sexually molested, he told his advisers that it was time to implement their plan, soon to be dubbed Operation Just Cause. Right after the stroke of midnight on December 20, 20,000 U.S. troops invaded Panama. Bush spent hours on the telephone calling Latin American leaders to mute any opposition to the use of military force in the region. Within nine hours, the U.S. military was in control of the country and the Panamanian political opposition that should have been elected in May 1989 was installed as the new government. Only twenty-four U.S. servicemen lost their lives in the largest American military operation since the end of the Vietnam War. Noriega, however, was nowhere to be found. Over the course of four humiliating days, American troops looked for him until he turned up seeking asylum at the residence of the papal representative in Panama City. "Finding Noriega made our Christmas," Barbara Bush wrote in her diary. When the Vatican could not decide what to do with him, the U.S. military set up huge speakers and began blasting hard rock music twenty-four hours a day into the compound. Finally, on January 3, 1990, Noriega gave himself up to U.S. authorities and was flown to Florida to face trial.

Noriega's defeat was only the first of Bush's successes in the first half of 1990. In the heady days after border controls ended between the two Germanies, even Chancellor Helmut Kohl assumed that reunification would take between five and ten years. On November 28, 1989, without consulting his own foreign minister, let alone Washington, Kohl had put on record a ten-point plan for merging the two Germanies, which would follow elections in East Germany that were expected sometime in late 1990 or early 1991. But in the wake of the revolutions happening around them in east-central Europe, the East German people refused to wait that long for their first chance at a free election since 1933. Initially they had reacted to the open frontier by fleeing in large numbers for West Germany, where they could earn four or five times as much. By January 1990, 1 percent of the population of East Germany had fled. Then East German public opinion shifted. The people decided to stay and try to change East Germany from within. The elections took place on March 18, 1990, and to the surprise of every chancellery and intelligence service in NATO and the

Warsaw Pact, the hastily formed conservative party alliance won 62 percent of the vote. The election results gave Bush's policy of hinging U.S. policy on the desires of the Germans themselves a huge boost, ending any remaining opposition from Great Britain and the French to rapid unification and left Gorbachev resigned to the disappearance of East Germany, though not yet to its absorption into NATO.

Under U.S. leadership, the diplomatic structure for managing the unification of Germany had also changed in the first months of 1990. Bush deflected Soviet, British, and French pressures to have the four victorious powers from World War II—Great Britain, France, the Soviet Union, and the United States—determine the destiny of the two Germanies, with little or no German input. He and Scowcroft preferred that the two Germanies decide these questions themselves but reluctantly accepted the fact that the four powers had to play a role. Bush wanted Moscow's 380,000 troops to leave eastern Germany forever; and he worried that Anglo-French fears of a united Germany and Soviet fears of losing East Germany to NATO would lead to an unacceptable compromise. At the recommendation of the State Department, Bush approved the idea of "two-plus-four" talks—the two Germanies plus the four World War II victors—which James Baker presented to the Soviet, French, and British foreign ministers. East and West Germany would decide the internal matters associated with unification, while the four powers discussed external issues, including security guarantees to a unified Germany's neighbors and the still-sensitive question of the 650-mile German-Polish border, which had been shifted westward in 1945 and was the source of unresolved claims on both sides. The French, British, and Soviets accepted this approach in February 1990, with the talks to begin following the East German elections. They would prove to be a confidence-building measure for all parties concerned.

In the wake of the surprise election victory for the West in East

Germany, George Bush's management of Gorbachev faced a severe challenge from within the USSR itself. The Baltic republics—Estonia, Latvia, and Lithuania—were ripe for the same political explosion as eastern Europe. In late February the Lithuanians had also voted for democratic civil society and expected staunch support from George Bush. On March 11 the newly elected Lithuanian parliament declared Lithuania's independence, putting Bush in a very difficult position. Whereas the United States had recognized East Germany in the early 1970s, it had never formally recognized the incorporation of the three Baltic republics into the USSR in 1941.

Even before the elections in Lithuania, Bush had decided he would have to respond to reform in the Baltics differently from that in eastern Europe. He had told Gorbachev at Malta that despite its formal position, the United States would treat Lithuania as an internal matter of the USSR so long as Gorbachev promised not to use force in the republic and agreed that eventually the principle of self-determination should be extended there. This was a private understanding that reflected some inescapable realities. The United States had no way to protect Lithuania should the Soviets decide to deploy their forces to quell the separatist movement. But it also reflected a judgment call by Bush about the nature of reform in the Soviet Union. Ultimately the survival of Baltic independence would require a revolution in the way that the Kremlin understood its sphere of influence. The only revolutionary in Moscow with any sway was Gorbachev. This meant tough love for Lithuanian democrats in the short run and a hide of steel against critics who would be sure to see the contradiction in Bush's policy.

In the wake of the Lithuanian declaration of independence, it appeared that Gorbachev was unwilling or unable to hold up his end of his bargain with Bush. On March 26 Soviet troops took control of some government buildings in Vilnius, the Lithuanian capital, and started looking for young Lithuanians who refused to appear for duty in the Soviet army. In response, Bush and Baker stood alone in the administration in wanting to continue to tilt toward Gorbachev. Scowcroft and Cheney preferred a tougher line, but Bush overruled them.

The Bush administration swallowed hard and decided that the future of European security depended on keeping Gorbachev in charge of Soviet policy long enough to effect the unification of Germany and a pullback of Soviet troops from Europe. To the disappointment of bipartisan majorities in the U.S. House and Senate, as well as to many in the media, the administration muted its criticism of Soviet policy in Lithuania while using back channels to get the two sides to talk. The administration sent Senator Richard Lugar of Indiana as an unofficial envoy to Vilnius to recommend to the Lithuanians that their best strategy in the short term was to keep the Soviets talking.

Viewed from the capitals of Europe and Washington, the wisdom of Bush's calculation seemed unclear. Outwardly Soviet policy was tightening on all issues. Even Eduard Shevardnadze, Gorbachev's liberal-minded foreign minister, was dismissing a united Germany in NATO as impossible. Meanwhile the Soviet military was playing a greater role in arms control discussions, meaning that Moscow was backtracking.

When Gorbachev imposed a partial energy embargo on the breakaway republic in late April 1990, pressure built for U.S. sanctions against Moscow in the style of those initiated by President Jimmy Carter in 1980, after the invasion of Afghanistan. In addition to the politically deft Baltic-American lobby, Bush faced widespread opposition from idealists and realists alike. The conservative columnist George Will wrote acidly that the Lithuanian crisis proved that "Bushism is Reaganism minus the passion for freedom." Meanwhile the grand old man of American realism, Richard Nixon, let the *New York Times* know that he feared Bush was making the same mistake as Reagan by identifying the continued political survival of Gorbachev with U.S. interests. The unkindest cut of all came from Lithuania's president, Vytautas Landsbergis, who in the face of the Soviet energy embargo assailed Bush for authoring a latter-day Munich, the twentieth century's symbol of wrongheaded appeasement. Meanwhile, contrary advice flowed from a very nervous West German government in Bonn, which privately urged Bush not to do anything that might trigger meaningful Soviet retaliation against the process of unification.

In response, Bush decided on a subtle two-pronged strategy to restrain Gorbachev, whom he was expected to meet in Washington in May. He wrote a confidential letter to the Soviet leader on April 29, reassuring him that he still hoped for a successful summit. At the same time he reminded Gorbachev of his promises at Malta and warned that unless a real dialogue began between Moscow and the Lithuanians, there was no way the U.S. government could accept a trade agreement with Moscow, which he knew that Gorbachev needed to give his people some economic hope. "I may be forced very soon to state publicly that under existing conditions there can be no trade agreement," Bush stated. "This is simply a statement of reality. It is not meant to be provocative." Bush emphasized for Gorbachev the domestic "flak" he was taking on the issue, informing him that because of the Lithuanian crisis the Senate was not going to ratify any trade agreement whatever he might say. Bush was once again extremely frank about his strategy: "I have often stated publicly, not only my desire to see perestroika succeed, but also to see you personally prevail. I still feel very strongly about that."

While carefully applying pressure to Gorbachev, Bush overruled his advisers in the State and Defense departments and decided to use a commencement address at Oklahoma State University to promise huge reform of NATO at its upcoming summit in July. Unlike his other pronouncements on European security, he had not tested this initiative with America's allies ahead of time. He also decided that the United States would advocate even greater cuts in the number of soldiers in Europe and would cancel the projected modernization of short-range nuclear missiles for NATO. The goal of this activism was to increase the odds that Gorbachev could accept a united Germany within NATO and an agreement to cut both sides' conventional forces in Europe. Once that happened, he believed, Americans would accept that their president's temporary abandonment of freedom in the Baltics had been a calculated risk in the service of a larger goal.

Bush knew that he had put his place in history on the line. Privately he told Condoleezza Rice, a Soviet specialist on the staff of the National Security Council, "I don't want people to look back 20 or 40 years from now and say, 'That's where everything went off track. That's where progress stopped.' " As it turned out, Bush had correctly assessed his Soviet partner. Gorbachev was himself facing enormous pressure to forcibly overturn Lithuanian independence. To calm the remaining totalitarians in the Communist Party, Gorbachev had permitted the drafting of a plan to establish military control over the republic, while looking for measures far short of that. The beleaguered Soviet leader believed that Lithuanians would stay within the USSR and hoped that by imposing economic hardship on them they would drop independence as too risky. In 1956 Khrushchev had launched the invasion of Hungary when he became convinced that the West was taking advantage of his weaknesses. Bush gave none of Gorbachev's challengers any fresh evidence that this was happening again.

Bush understood that the U.S. government would have to speak with one voice on Gorbachev. Ronald Reagan would occasionally make a tough speech that undermined the diplomatic efforts of his secretary of state George Shultz. The Reagan speechwriting team had a group of skeptics, and the State Department could not fight every battle for the new approach. Knowing that Gorbachev and his opponents in Moscow read these speeches—the Soviet leader

used to complain to Shultz about Reagan's hard-line addresses—
Bush exercised greater control over the rhetoric of his own administration. Cheney, who remained deeply skeptical of Gorbachev,
was not permitted to speak his mind publicly.

Since the fall of 1989, Bush's empathy for Gorbachev had deepened. He now grasped better than most in Washington that Gorbachev's perestroika had become a high-wire act. The Soviet leader
was surrounded by a cadre of true reformers, some of whom already doubted their own commitment to communism, but with
the exception of Gorbachev and his foreign minister, Eduard Shevardnadze, these men lacked power. Indeed, the Communist Party
was still dominated by hard-liners whose goals—a higher standard
of living for the Soviet people but not at the cost of losing the empire to the West—the Pentagon and many in the CIA continued in-
correctly to associate with Gorbachev. Gorbachev, in fact, called
these hard-liners the "conservative colossus." And whereas Gorbachev's advisers were divided as to how to deal with this colossus,
he was determined to defeat them through the Communist Party.
If he left the party, as some of his team recommended, Gorbachev
feared he would lack the levers necessary to accomplish his massive reforms. Bush also had an intuitive understanding that Gorbachev's own ideological transformation was incomplete, which
explained some of the contradictions in his actions. The Soviet
leader remained committed to a communist future and could not
accept that Marxism-Leninism was a spent force; so he kept pushing reforms that wouldn't work, yet he was too much of a humanitarian to crack down when things failed. Bush decided that it was
in U.S. interests to hold his hand—keep him in power and encourage him—as he unwillingly dismantled the Soviet empire, at home
as well as abroad.

The wisdom of this approach became clear at the Bush-
Gorbachev meeting in Washington on May 30, 1990. In one of the
most dramatic diplomatic about-faces in the history of U.S.-Soviet

summits, Gorbachev changed his mind and his country's policy on Germany on the spot and in front of his advisers. Bush set the scene by intentionally bringing up the contradiction between Gorbachev's rhetoric and his country's German policy. Gorbachev had already publicly admitted that a unified Germany was inevitable and talked about the self-determination of all Europeans but still refused to accept that a unified Germany could choose to join NATO. "I tried a new tack," Bush later recalled. "I reminded Gorbachev that the Helsinki Final Act [signed in 1975] stated that all countries had the right to choose their alliances. To me that meant Germany should be able to decide for itself what it wanted. Did he agree?" Gorbachev stunned everyone by shrugging his shoulders and saying "yes." At the insistence of an aide, who furiously sent him a note, Bush asked Gorbachev to repeat what he had just said. "I agree," said Gorbachev, "to say so publicly, that the United States and the USSR are in favor of seeing a united Germany, with a final settlement leaving it up to where a united Germany can choose." Bush then stated the American corollary to the dramatic concession by Gorbachev: "We support a united Germany in NATO. If they do not want in, we will respect that." "I agree," answered Gorbachev. At that moment, Bush judged that he had to reward the Soviets. Taking Gorbachev aside, he privately told him that he would get his trade agreement. All Bush asked was that Gorbachev should help him with Congress by lightening up the pressure on Lithuania.

Bush was at his most decisive in May 1990. His push to ensure that a unified Germany would join NATO coincided with a requirement that he manage his most difficult domestic challenge, the burgeoning budget deficit. Indeed, on May 4, the day that he announced in Oklahoma the U.S. commitment to transforming NATO into more of a political alliance, he privately decided that he would have to raise taxes at home to deal with the massive budget deficit left by Ronald Reagan. At the end of that day, after draining a well-earned cocktail, he dictated the calm he felt despite the challenges: "I'm tired, relaxed though—maybe it's the martini—but convinced we're on the right track in the big picture, [though I] am wondering how long the public will support me."

Whereas events seemed to follow no particular timetable in Europe, at home Bush faced an inescapable deadline. Estimates of the budget deficit in the next fiscal year had ballooned from $111 billion to $171 billion, or more than 4 percent of gross domestic product. The numbers had actually been worse in the mid-1980s, but in 1985 Congress had passed Gramm-Rudman-Hollings, which required that the federal government take drastic steps to restore balance in its accounts. If the deficit were not lowered to $64 billion by October 1, the start of the 1991 fiscal year, an automatic scythe would lop 40 percent off every account in the federal budget, including defense, housing, and medical expenditures.

Bush tried to deal with this approaching budget emergency as if it were a foreign policy problem. His instinct was to reach out to fellow leaders and work the issue. As ever, he preferred that these talks occur in secret. And although some of his defenders would later say that the president would be caught by surprise by the rancor that the process caused, from the start he knew that the stakes were high and that he faced a challenge from his own party. "If we handle it wrong," Bush wrote in his diary, "our troops will rebel on taxes—everybody will rebel on social security benefits—and there will be no deal at all, and we need a deal." Bush also expected that he would have to break his no-tax pledge at some point, but he wanted a little help from the other side. "I'm willing to eat crow," he wrote in May 1990, "but the others are going to have to eat crow. I'll have to yield on 'Read My Lips,' and they're going to have to yield on some of their rhetoric on taxes and on entitlements."

Whether due to naïveté, renewed self-confidence, or arrogance, Bush assumed that his personal charm, his honesty, and his sense of a mutual interest in good government would suppress his opponents' interest in seeing him hurt politically. He had worked with many of the Democrats before, as a congressman in the 1960s and most recently as Ronald Reagan's advocate for tax reform. Some personal friendships could possibly play in Bush's favor, too, especially that with Dan Rostenkowski of Illinois, who headed the House Ways and Means Committee. Some of Bush's advisers objected that he should not involve himself personally in the inevitable horse-trading with the Democrats, but Bush insisted on his approach. Curiously, no one in the White House had thought about a strategy for ensuring that the rank and file of the Republican Party would accept whatever deal emerged. Everyone just assumed they would go along.

Thus George H. W. Bush for a moment, at least, became a great president. In the late spring of 1990, as he risked his international prestige to slow events in the Baltics long enough to permit the inclusion of a united Germany in NATO, he threw himself into negotiating a bipartisan compromise at home that would heal the open budget sore. In each case Bush sacrificed short-term personal political gain for what he considered in the national interest. Neither decision was easy for him, but they both reflected an instinctive sense of the direction he ought to take. And the direction would be proved right.

Bush did not enjoy the same unconditional success with his domestic negotiating partners as he had with the Soviets. The Democratic leaders had insisted that there be no "preconditions" before starting the negotiations, and Bush agreed, knowing that this meant taxes were on the table though he had not yet publicly broken his pledge. But the negotiations soon got bogged down, and the party leaders insisted on increasing the number of negotiators to satisfy their own factions. By late June a fatigue had set in, and Bush sensed the need to issue some kind of joint statement that indicated the talks were having some success. In a haphazard meeting on

June 26, Majority Leader Mitchell managed to get Bush to agree to a short statement indicating that both sides agreed that "tax revenue increases" would form part of an eventual budget deal. The type of tax increase, whether on income or on services, was not specified. But the fact that these words appeared in the statement made public what Bush had privately known for some time, that he would break his chief campaign pledge.

The moment the statement was posted in the White House Press Office, Bush received more criticism than praise. Conservatives like Chief of Staff John Sununu, Vice President Quayle, and Secretary of Agriculture Clayton Yeutter warned that the effect of breaking this promise would be devastating on support from the Reaganite base. Moderates rallied to Bush, but they counted for little in the Republican Party of the 1990s. From the sidelines, Richard Nixon wrote Bush to soften the blow, saying, "The mark of a great leader is to change his policies to meet new situations even when that means backing away from a campaign commitment. As you know I had to burn a lot of my own speeches and eat a lot of words when I went to China in 1972."

Ironically, this harsh political criticism from American conservatives for showing too much realism at home coincided with George H. W. Bush achieving one of the greatest foreign policy victories of any U.S. president in peacetime. The summer of 1990 brought the undeniable end of the Cold War, as it ushered in the final phase of creating the new Europe that Bush and Helmut Kohl, practically alone, had believed possible that year. As Bush had promised Gorbachev in early May, the North Atlantic Treaty Organization decided at its July meeting to put the alliance on a new footing, and for the first time observers from the Warsaw Pact were invited. Having been given this useful political cover, Gorbachev then publicly admitted the end of the Kremlin's traditional policy on Germany, formally telling Kohl that if a united Germany chose to join the Western alliance, Moscow would not object. References to the end of the Cold War now started to appear in George Bush's speeches. How far this new relationship with Moscow would go remained unclear, but in a few weeks a surprising event in the Middle East would give Bush a magnificent opportunity to test Gorbachev's willingness to complete the transformation from adversary to ally.

5

Commander in Chief

George Bush's greatest challenge as president came in a region of the world where the United States and not the Soviet Union had held sway in the Cold War. As Bush tried to manage the politics of Soviet decline, a border dispute was heating up between the Arab nations of Iraq and Kuwait. Iraqi nationalists had long considered the oil-rich sheikhdom on Iraq's southern border to be the country's nineteenth province. In 1961 the regime of Abdul Qassim had threatened to invade when Kuwait declared its independence from Great Britain. Baghdad's petulance produced a show of force by the British navy, long the traditional protector of the tiny oil emirates in the Persian Gulf. A generation later, Iraqi president Saddam Hussein launched a campaign of intimidation to force a negotiation over control of the Rumaila oil fields that straddled the international border.

From the perspective of most in the Bush administration, Saddam was certainly misbehaving—no key American policymaker doubted he was a thug—but he still did not pose a threat to the balance of power in the region. The Iran-Iraq war, which ended in stalemate in 1988, had left Iraq with huge debts, a broken economy, and an urgent need for civil reconstruction. The U.S. intelligence community thought differently, but its increasingly direct warnings about Saddam's expansionist intentions fell on deaf ears.

Distracted by the fast-paced events in eastern Europe and convinced of the wisdom of engagement with the Iraqi dictator, the
Bush administration sluggishly reexamined its policy of using Iraq
to balance Iran. Besides the CIA, pressures were building in James
Baker's inner circle at the State Department to switch to a policy
of containing Iraqi power, but these pressures led nowhere until
Saddam made his big move.

As July turned to August and Saddam Hussein massed troops
along Iraq's border with Kuwait, Bush repeatedly reached out to his
Arab friends in the Middle East for their counsel. Neither of the
two things that the president learned from these telephone calls
proved helpful. The Arab leaders—Hosni Mubarak of Egypt, King
Fahd of Saudi Arabia, and King Hussein of Jordan—were confident that Saddam was bluffing. He was just flexing his muscle to
get more from the Kuwaitis. And the Arab moderates were equally
confident that the worst thing Bush could do was to meddle in this
intra-Arab dispute. Let the Arabs settle it themselves, they advised.

"On the morning of August 2, Barbara and I were still in bed with
the papers when Brent [Scowcroft] arrived just before 5:00 A.M.,"
Bush later wrote in his diary. The night before, Bush had received reports on the movement of Iraqi troops across the border. The U.S.
ambassador to Kuwait, Nathaniel Howell, had sent a cable reporting
sounds of gunfire in Kuwait City and then passing along the ruling
Al-Sabah family's request for military assistance. Then after midnight the United Nations had begun debating a resolution to condemn Iraq and demand its unconditional withdrawal from Kuwaiti
territory. Bush had preferred to wait for morning to see where things
stood. With the early morning confirmation from Scowcroft that
with a force of 120,000 troops and 850 tanks Saddam had swallowed all of Kuwait, Bush's first decision was to sign an order freez-
ing all Iraqi and Kuwaiti assets and then to order American warships
to the Persian Gulf. Beyond that, he was quite fatalistic. "There is
little the U.S. can do in a situation like this," he believed.

A trip to Aspen, Colorado, had already been scheduled for later in the day, where Bush was to join British prime minister Margaret Thatcher in a public discussion of the future of NATO after the Cold War. Since Thatcher was already in Colorado, Bush decided not to cancel the trip because he needed to confer with her on Saddam's move. Before leaving Washington, Bush decided to hold an early morning NSC meeting.

The meeting did not go well on many levels. When Bush entered the Cabinet Room at 7:30 A.M., it was full of press for a pre-meeting photo opportunity. He gave a prepared statement and then took questions. The opening statement was straightforward; Bush called on Saddam to withdraw immediately and unconditionally, and he left no doubt of what he thought of the Iraqi act, labeling it "naked aggression." But on the critical issue of what the world's strongest military power was prepared to do, Bush had little to say. In response to a question about the possibility of U.S. military action, he offered a mouthful of words that many misinterpreted as a sign of passivity or resignation: "We're not discussing intervention. I would not discuss any military options even if we'd agreed upon them." The words were accurate, but with so many quick to see this president as weak and indecisive, Bush needed to project self-assurance. This he failed to do.

The problems did not exit the room with the press. Most of Bush's advisers were even more uncertain of the nature of this crisis than he. A general fatalistic malaise had settled on all of his top aides, with the singular exception of Brent Scowcroft. Baker was in the Soviet Union, and though Cheney disliked Saddam, he and Colin Powell, the chairman of the Joint Chiefs of Staff, were not thinking in terms of a U.S. military response. Indeed, there was no discussion in the National Security Council of ridding Kuwait of the Iraqis. Instead there seemed to be a grudging acceptance that Iraq's absorption of Kuwait was at least for now an unfortunate fact of life. "I was frankly appalled," Scowcroft wrote later. The only action the group could agree on was to press for an international oil embargo to penalize Saddam in the hope that he might abandon this adventure.

Although Bush was not thinking of any military crusades, he was determined to use the crisis to continue building a better world. He told his advisers to start drafting a joint U.S.-Soviet statement condemning the invasion that Baker might get Shevardnadze and Gorbachev to accept. If Moscow went along with it, this would be unprecedented. Iraq had been a Soviet ally since the overthrow of King Faisal II in July 1958, and Moscow was the principal source of Iraqi weaponry. Bush also wanted to enlist the Soviets to join the French (the second most important arms suppliers to Baghdad) in an arms embargo to accompany the oil embargo. That the president had not given up on Kuwaiti sovereignty was clear from a third decision Bush made. The United States would not close its embassies in Baghdad or Kuwait City, in part to monitor the safety of the 3,800 U.S. citizens in Kuwait and the 500 Americans living in Iraq. Finally, Bush wanted to prevent Iraq from moving farther south into Saudi Arabia.

After making several telephone calls to allies from Air Force One, Bush met Thatcher in Aspen. She was resolved to do something for Kuwait. "If Iraq wins, no small state is safe," she told Bush. Thatcher's words were a tonic for the president, who readily agreed. Up to that point he had been getting little encouragement for the United States to show any initiative. President Mubarak and King Hussein had just told him that they still believed an Arab solution was possible. The reaction of the Saudis was different but no more helpful. King Fahd was much more suspicious of Saddam than the other Arab leaders. "He is following Hitler in creating world problems—with a difference: one was conceited and one is both conceited and crazy," Fahd told Bush during their telephone call. "I believe nothing will work with Saddam but the use of force." Yet when Bush asked the Saudi ruler whether he would like the United States to station warplanes in the kingdom, Fahd declined, apparently more nervous about an American deployment than an Iraqi attack. Thatcher was not, however, the sole helpful ally at the moment. From James Baker, who was in Mongolia, having just met with Shevardnadze in Siberia, there were hints that the joint statement with the Soviets might happen. And, on August 3, this historic act of U.S.-Soviet cooperation occurred.

Returning to Washington early in the morning of August 3, Bush had made up his mind that Saddam's intentions were too uncertain to take any more risks in the Gulf. On August 4, he decided to send 100,000 U.S. ground forces to Saudi Arabia if the Saudis agreed, and the next day he dispatched Cheney to Riyadh to change King Fahd's mind about accepting a U.S. containment force. Meanwhile the White House was on tenterhooks. It would take forty-eight hours for the initial 10,000 of these troops to arrive, and U.S. intelligence had already detected the movement of Iraqi troops to the Saudi border. Yet the intelligence was frustratingly fragmentary. Lacking any human agents, U.S. intelligence had to wait for the next pass of the one available American spy satellite to get better pictures of the scene at the border.

The more Bush thought about the significance of what had happened in the Gulf, the more he came to share Thatcher and Scowcroft's conviction that there was more at stake in the Gulf than the defense of Saudi Arabia. Bush was not a conceptual thinker. He had a sense of appropriate goals and appropriate means of attaining those goals. It was the thinking he had done in response to recent events in Europe that helped him frame U.S. choices in the Gulf. For a year he and Gorbachev had been communicating about a new international system, where military force would play less of a role and in which the superpowers shared in the responsibility for keeping the peace. It didn't make sense for Saddam to be allowed to do what no one else could. Moreover, border revisionism was in the air in 1990. Shops in Budapest were selling maps of Greater Hungary, which contained parts of present-day Yugoslavia, Romania, and Czechoslovakia. In March fighting had broken out in Hungarian-speaking Transylvania. Although the Germans seemed to be satisfied with their eastern borders, what would prevent a less pro-European German regime in the future from following Saddam's example? Bush understood that the entire world was in play and that many future expansionists would be watching how the great powers dealt with Saddam.

The next phase of Bush's handling of the Gulf crisis would be marked with the same elements of secrecy and surprise as his selection of Dan Quayle as his running mate and his initial decision to drop his "no new taxes" pledge. Bush knew that he had to decide whether to stake American prestige on changing the facts on the ground in Kuwait. It was easy for Margaret Thatcher to huff and puff. Britain was too weak to do anything of consequence to Saddam. The United States, however, had the power to make a difference. Bush mulled things over without letting any of his advisers know where this process was heading. It was characteristic of Bush that he preferred to let the wheels turn secretly. When he was ready to act, he would let people know.

"The enormity of Iraq is upon me now," he confided to his private diary on Sunday, August 5, three days after the invasion of Kuwait. Leaving his helicopter on the South Lawn of the White House that afternoon, Bush let his advisers and the world know his decision. "This will not stand, this aggression against Kuwait," he announced, delighting Scowcroft but worrying the rest of his team. In one phrase George Bush had committed the United States to reversing the Iraqi invasion of Kuwait. At this moment, Bush did not know how this goal would be achieved, but he suspected that it might well require the use of force. General Powell lost no time in cautioning the president that a war with Iraq "would be the NFL, not a scrimmage." When Baker returned from the Soviet Union he asked Bush whether he understood the political risk that he had just taken. "I know you're aware of the fact that this has all the ingredients that brought down three of the last five Presidents: a hostage crisis, body bags, and a full-fledged economic recession caused by forty-dollar oil."

"I know that, Jimmy, I know that," Bush replied. "But we're doing what's right; we're doing what is clearly in the national interest of the United States. Whatever else happens, so be it." Doing what's right was going to be very expensive, so Bush sent Baker around the world, on what became known as the "tin-cup" tour, to raise money from allies for the U.S. deployment in the Gulf. Ultimately the effort was so successful that the United States would make a profit on the war. Thirty-three countries would join the coalition, including Egypt, Syria, Saudi Arabia, and five other Arab states.

Bush's determination had an immediate human cost. There were an estimated 2,000 westerners still in Iraq and Kuwait, of whom nearly half were American. Since the invasion many westerners had managed to leave, but in response to the hard line taken by Bush and Thatcher the Iraqi government had begun to hold some against their will, calling them a "human shield." Meanwhile, Iraqi soldiers had surrounded the U.S. and British embassies, making the diplomats virtual hostages.

It is rare that a consensus develops among a president's advisers in a crisis. Some presidents are passive and the choice is made by others, but in the end someone has to choose. Dwight Eisenhower had to make up his own mind during the two Middle Eastern crises of his administration, in 1956 and 1958, although he did rely heavily on Secretary of State John Foster Dulles. Similarly, John F. Kennedy's Executive Committee did not produce an up-or-down policy recommendation on what to do in the Cuban missile crisis. It would be the same for Bush. He assembled his closest foreign policy advisers, forming the Gang of Eight, and after listening to them hash out the issues he would choose what to do. From the start, Bush faced divided counsel. Scowcroft and Cheney generally supported the use of force; Baker and Powell generally counseled patience to let tough talk and sanctions compel Saddam to leave Kuwait. Vice President Quayle, Chief of Staff John Sununu, Scowcroft's assistant Robert Gates, and the undersecretary of defense for policy, Paul Wolfowitz, also participated, but their views were far less influential. Bush's first significant decisions were to assure Saddam that he would not be allowed to keep Kuwait and, after receiving a reluctant green light from Fahd, to send 100,000 U.S. troops to Saudi Arabia so that the Iraqis could not move into the kingdom. The mission to defend Saudi Arabia became known as Operation Desert Shield.

• • •

The need for more major decisions came fast. On August 2 the United Nations had passed Resolution 660, condemning the invasion and demanding an Iraqi withdrawal from Kuwait. A few days later the world body approved placing economic sanctions on Iraq but did not fully authorize member states to enforce them. On August 18 came the news that five Iraqi oil tankers were heading to the port of Aden in Yemen, a report that posed a dilemma for the Gang of Eight. Bush, Cheney, Scowcroft, and even Powell believed that the U.S. Navy could and should fire on the tankers under Article 51 of the UN charter, which gives member states the right to use force in self-defense. James Baker, however, lobbied the president hard not to use this authority when there was a possibility of getting a specific resolution that authorized "all means necessary" to enforce the blockade. Baker, who was working closely with Shevardnadze, believed that Moscow might also accept the naval enforcement of the trade embargo, if the United States waited to get UN authorization. Bush shared Baker's enthusiasm for making the Soviets a key partner in the coalition, but he worried about what lesson Saddam would take from seeing the tankers get through the U.S. naval blockade.

Bush also heard from Thatcher on the matter. She shared the president's concern about a leaky embargo but was far less committed to using the UN in this crisis. She saw only potential difficulties in going back to the UN for additional resolutions and was not concerned about the Soviet response. When Bush explained to her the possible rationale for letting the tankers go through, Thatcher taunted him, "Well, all right, George, but this is no time to go wobbly."

Thatcher had needled the president in a particularly sensitive spot. Nevertheless, Bush saw the broader, strategic wisdom in Baker's recommendation and instructed the secretary of state to give Moscow until August 25 to sign on to a new UN resolution enforcing sanctions. In the meantime, the U.S. Navy would monitor the tanker without interfering. "I think they want to be included," he had written a few days earlier about the Soviets in his diary, "and they don't want to always be the last one to know. They want some standing, some face, and it's so important in the world . . . if they see us go rushing in carrying the ball and they have no role, then they just look like bit players or unimportant." This turned out to be a good risk to take. After Gorbachev made another failed attempt to get Saddam to realize the trouble he was in, Soviet diplomats joined the other permanent members in the Security Council in passing the UN resolution that Bush wanted. In the meantime the tankers had reached Yemen, but with its broader objective achieved, Washington no longer cared.

· · ·

At the end of World War II, Franklin Roosevelt spoke about how the five great powers could cooperate for peace. Having witnessed the failure of the League of Nations to deter Italian, Japanese, and German aggression in the 1930s, Roosevelt wanted the great powers to give the world body that emerged from the war some real teeth. For this reason China, France, Great Britain, the Soviet Union, and the United States were made permanent members of the Security Council. The five were also given vetoes, and for Roosevelt's concept to work the five would have to agree. But they didn't, and with the exception of 1950, when Stalin's miscalculation (the Soviets temporarily boycotted the UN) allowed the Security Council to condemn North Korea's invasion of South Korea and establish a UN force under U.S. leadership, the UN had been practically useless as a bulwark against aggression. Few Americans had more hands-on knowledge of the limitations of the UN than George Bush, but his brief stint there had also left him with positive feelings about the institution. It was a happy accident of history that this former UN ambassador was now a head of state at a time when the United Nations could matter.

While fishing off Kennebunkport in late August, Bush and Scowcroft mused about this remarkable opportunity to pick up where Roosevelt had left off in 1945. The joint statement of August 3 and the tanker decision signaled a sea change in U.S.-Soviet relations, opening the possibility for even greater cooperation. The fish were not biting, and Scowcroft suggested the phrase "new world order" to describe the collective security system that might be emerging. Bush liked the phrase and decided he would use it publicly, but not before seeing Gorbachev to discuss how the two countries might deepen their cooperation in the Gulf. After returning to Washington, the president drafted a letter to Gorbachev suggesting a short meeting in a neutral capital. Gorbachev accepted, and the men decided to meet in Helsinki on September 9. Meanwhile the State Department drafted yet another joint statement for Bush to suggest to the Soviets—this one showing Soviet support for the use of force if Saddam refused to leave Kuwait.

• • •

In the late summer of 1990, however much he would have wanted to, Bush did not have the luxury of spending all of his time on foreign policy. The budget negotiations were stalled, and Washington faced the draconian Gramm-Rudman-Hollings deadline on October 1. After privately deciding in May that he would have to accept "revenue enhancements," new taxes, to get the Democratic-controlled Congress to accept a budget agreement, Bush signaled in June his willingness to abandon his "no new taxes" pledge as part of a comprehensive approach to reducing federal spending. Concerned about this deadline, Bush asked House and Senate negotiators to work through the summer, but the Democratic leadership refused, blaming the midterm elections for the need to allow legislators to go home in August.

There were three sides in the discussion, and all were far apart. The Bush team wanted to reduce the deficit by increasing taxes on tobacco and alcoholic beverages, and by reducing some of the federal government's subsidies for health care for the elderly (Medicare). With the economy teetering on the edge of recession, the administration was still hoping to spur on business activity with a lowering of capital gains taxes. For their part, Democratic leaders Senator George Mitchell and House Speaker Thomas Foley wanted to close the budgetary gap by raising taxes on the wealthiest Americans and increasing gasoline taxes, noting that American motorists paid a fraction of what their counterparts in other industrial countries paid. In addition, Democrats believed that higher gasoline taxes would create incentives for energy diversification and efficiency. The Republicans in Congress formed the third bloc in this discussion, but they could not agree on what they wanted.

With the Gulf crisis looming and the summit only a few days away, Bush was looking to catch a break in these difficult budget talks. "I just hope that Iraq and the country's unity can now be parlayed into support for the budget agreement," he confided to his diary. At Andrews Air Force Base, where congressional leaders and the White House's budget team were locked in negotiations, Bush made the pitch for bipartisanship in a time of peril, before leaving for Helsinki to meet with Gorbachev.

The Helsinki summit turned out to be a dream compared to what was happening back home. Bush's tactic of showing empathy to the Soviet reformers worked like a charm. He immediately set the tone by overturning forty years of U.S. policy in the Middle East. "The press asked me," Bush said to Gorbachev, "if I would ask you to send forces. I said I had no such plans, but I tell you that if you so decide, I have no problems with that." With this offer, Bush proved to the embattled Gorbachev that he believed in cooperation. "The world order I see coming out of this is U.S. and Soviet cooperation to solve not only this but other problems in the Middle East," Bush added. "I want to work with you as equal partners in dealing with this." This offer to accept Soviet troops in the Middle East was an unwanted surprise for Scowcroft, who winced but was delighted when Gorbachev said no.

Bush had wisely chosen to start the meeting by disarming Gorbachev. The Soviet leader had come to Helsinki with a dangerous proposal cooked up by the Arabists in the Soviet foreign ministry, who had not given up on helping Iraq. Some in Moscow wanted the coalition to offer Saddam a deal. In exchange for releasing the hostages, pulling out of Kuwait, and restoring the Al-Sabah regime, Iraq would receive a noninvasion pledge from Washington, a reduction in U.S. forces in Saudi Arabia, and their eventual replacement by an Arab peacekeeping force. The kicker was that the United States would eventually promise an international conference on the Middle East. This was exactly what Saddam hoped for. He wanted to be able to show that he had linked his dispute with Kuwait to the Arab-Israeli conflict. Bush revealed to Gorbachev his underlying concerns about Saddam's power, which would remain intact were he given this deal. "He still has his nuclear program and can return to aggression as soon as the U.S. leaves," he told the Soviet leader.

Bush patiently explained that he would not accept the Soviet deal for Saddam, but privately assured Gorbachev that once the

Kuwaiti crisis was solved, the United States would join the Soviets in sponsoring a Mideast peace conference. Gorbachev was delighted to hear that U.S. diplomats would work side by side with Soviet diplomats in the Middle East. By the end of the Helsinki summit, the Soviets accepted the language of a new U.S.-Soviet joint declaration supporting the use of "all means" against Saddam if he did not withdraw. Bush got what he needed to apply more pressure to Saddam and at no actual cost to American interests. Franklin Roosevelt would have been impressed.

· · ·

Over the course of the fall, Bush's assessment of the situation in the Gulf shifted dramatically. Implicit in the way he had turned down the Soviet proposal was a new level of intolerance for Saddam. Reports of Iraqi atrocities in Kuwait, some of which were provided by the human rights organization Amnesty International, personalized the conflict for Bush. Iraqis apparently had raided Kuwaiti hospitals and tossed infants out of incubators before sending the devices north. Rape was also apparently widespread in Kuwait City. Although some of these stories were later found to be false, Bush believed them, and the effect on his thinking cannot be exaggerated. He would refer to them again and again in his diary and personal letters. And, as a result, he privately began to expand his war aims. It would not be enough simply to eject Saddam from Kuwait; he now wanted him out of power.

Simultaneous with this hardening of his attitude toward Saddam emerged Bush's belief that domestic support for dealing with Iraq was a wasting asset. Following the Helsinki summit, he had unveiled the concept of the *new world order* in a speech to a joint session of Congress, in which he returned to the importance of bipartisanship. But the polls were showing an increase in criticism of U.S. policy in the Gulf. Although there was still strong support for the Bush approach, opposition had more than tripled, to 23 percent.

"It used to be 7%," Bush wrote, "and I worry, worry, worry about eroded support."

Bush viewed the home front in the Gulf crisis through the lens of Vietnam. He had seen how a lack of public support had torn the country and its military apart twenty years earlier, and he did not want to see that happen again. "Eroded support" was not a matter of whether people liked him, but whether they would allow his administration to do what was in the United States' national interest. Although Bush did not share the Pentagon's anxiety about deploying troops in a foreign conflict, the Vietnam scar that he still carried was the fear that public opinion could turn dramatically against the policy.

By late September Bush's concern would begin to manifest itself in presidential impatience to resolve the situation in the Gulf as quickly as possible. On September 22, after the Iraqis raided diplomatic residences in Kuwait, taking the U.S. consul hostage, Bush wondered whether "we need to speed up the timetable."

In this ominous environment Bush decided to expend even more political capital at home to avert a simultaneous budget crisis. It was his greatest political risk to date, but faced with the possible shutdown of parts of the federal government during an international crisis, Bush felt he had no choice. In late September Bush's negotiators told the Democrats that the president would no longer insist on any capital gains reductions, so long as the Democrats dropped their demand that the top marginal rate be lifted from 28 percent to 31 percent. The Bush team was convinced that so long as marginal rates did not increase, they could hold their own right wing. They were also overconfident that they could use Bush's still-high approval rating to push the Democrats to concede more. The least confident member of the team was Bush himself. "If the strong numbers today can help us get a deal based on the fact that Congress does not want to be 'bashed' in front of the whole country, so much the better," he confided to his diary. "But inside, I don't feel over-confident or arrogant based on the polling numbers, at all." A week later as the budget talks continued, Bush's concern grew: "As long as the people are with us, I've got a good chance. But once there starts to be an erosion, they're going to do what Lyndon Johnson said: they painted their asses white and ran with the antelopes."

Bush relied on the assessments of Sununu and budget chief Richard Darman on what his own domestic political coalition would bear. Bush needed no such coaching on the international coalition. But his instincts at home were not as sound. "It is said of me," wrote the introspective Bush, "that I much prefer to work on international affairs. Well, I am fully engrossed in this international crisis, and I must say I enjoy working all parts of it and I get into much more detail than I do on the domestic scene. So I think the answer is I do prefer this, but I see the budget deal as very important." The budget deal, as worked out by the parties, initiated a whole range of restraints on federal spending, including on entitlements for veterans, students, farmers, and federal employees. It included an unprecedented enforceable cap on all federal discretionary spending and introduced a "pay as you go" system, meaning that any new congressional spending initiative had to be twinned with a tax increase or a spending reduction to pay for it. The deal did not increase personal income tax rates and included some investment incentives. The pain was shared, and the American people were the beneficiaries of a more responsible budgetary process. What Bush and his advisers did not count on was the revolt of the Right that followed the announcement of the budget deal on September 30.

The leader of this revolt was Representative Newt Gingrich of Georgia, then in his second year as minority whip. Gingrich's central insight was that Reaganite tactics, which had proved so successful at the presidential level, should be applied in Congress. The current Republican leaders in the House and the Senate—Bob

Michel and Bob Dole—were aging lions who were accustomed to being in the minority. Despite their partisan rhetoric, they generally sought bipartisan compromises in the end. Gingrich believed that Republicans had to act as if they already had a majority, and if the Democrats refused to go along with their Reaganite policies, then the American people, for whom those nostrums were popular, would punish the Democrats at the next election.

Gingrich's first act of rebellion was clever and devious. Despite having agreed to the budget deal in private, he refused to have his picture taken at the Rose Garden ceremony where Bush and the congressional leadership announced the deal on September 30. Gingrich had not revealed to any of his fellow Republican leaders that he intended to boycott the ceremony, and this symbolic act came as a shock to President Bush. In the days that followed, Gingrich moved from silent protest to public criticism. Under the banner of what he called "reform populist conservatism," Gingrich decried the budget agreement as antigrowth and vowed not to support it.

Bush made a rare speech from the Oval Office to sell the deal. "This is the first time in my presidency that I've made an appeal like this to you," Bush said to the nation on October 2. But Republicans in Congress took their cues from Gingrich, and the agreement passed with scant support from the president's own party. Whereas 218 of 246 House Democrats supported the bill, only 32 of the 168 Republicans did so. Richard Viguerie, the conservative activist who had helped put Ronald Reagan in the White House through the use of direct-mail appeals, summed up what some of the Reaganite bloc were thinking after Bush broke his antitax pledge: "The only core base [Bush] pays attention to is the Yale Alumni Association."

Bush felt betrayed by Gingrich, for having broken what Ronald Reagan had often called the Eleventh Commandment—Thou Shalt Not Speak Ill of a Fellow Republican. "You are killing us, you are just killing us," an emotional Bush confided to Gingrich and his wife at a cocktail party just after the House Republicans started their revolt. The president was right. His public approval rate plummeted in October to 52 percent.

As he had feared, Bush's political situation got worse with this abandonment. The Democrats saw the opportunity to toughen the deal in light of the fact that if it were to pass now Bush would need support from the Democratic Left. They now decided to reverse their concession on marginal rates. In control of both houses and seeing the president faltering in opinion polls, the Democrats had no reason to compromise. There were many on the left of the party who wished to restore some of the progressive elements of the tax code that had been eliminated in 1986 when the top rates were dropped from 50 to 28 percent. Over the course of October the budget deal began to look more and more like what the Democrats had wanted going into the negotiations but never thought they could achieve.

As this was going on, Bush convinced himself not only that the United States had to go to war with Saddam soon, but that it could achieve both the coalition's goal of liberating Kuwait and his private goal of getting rid of Saddam without a land war. Above all, Bush wanted action before support for confronting Saddam collapsed, abroad as well as at home. On October 1 the Pentagon briefed Bush at length on an air and ground strategy. It was clear that Colin Powell and his commander in Saudi Arabia, General Norman Schwarzkopf, were determined to delay as long as possible the use of military force. Word had filtered back that Bush was very interested in possibly using a devastating air assault to shock Saddam into leaving Kuwait. The Pentagon briefer tried to pour cold water on the effectiveness of such an option. The Pentagon briefer similarly attempted to discourage Scowcroft and Cheney, who were known to believe that only a U.S. ground attack could dislodge the Iraqis. The Pentagon briefer offered a suicide scenario in which the now 200,000 troops in Saudi Arabia would attack due north, directly into the fortified Iraqi defenses along the Kuwaiti border.

None of the participants was happy with the briefing. Cheney ridiculed the ground strategy as "Hey Diddle Diddle Up-the-Middle" and encouraged the Pentagon to consider attacking the Iraqis from the western desert, which borders on Jordan. Scowcroft, who also wanted more creative thinking, asked why the United States did not launch a left hook attack around the Iraqi occupation force to eventually cut it off from Baghdad. Both Cheney and Scowcroft believed that, in any case, any realistic plan would require the doubling of U.S. troops in Saudi Arabia.

As Scowcroft and Cheney pressed the military to come up with a real plan for a land war, Bush preferred to think in terms of how to deal a knockout blow to Saddam much sooner. He raised with his advisers the idea that the United States should provoke a quick air war with Saddam before Christmas. (Bush once again borrowed from Franklin Roosevelt's foreign policy playbook. In 1940 Roosevelt had ordered the coast guard to patrol farther from U.S. shores explicitly to draw fire from the German navy.) He had been thinking about the possibility that America would be provoked into war because of the reports of what Saddam was doing to the people of Kuwait and because of the Iraqi dictator's decision to take Western hostages. Now he wondered whether it might make sense to provoke Saddam first. "The news is saying some members of Congress feel I might use a minor incident to go to war, and they may be right," he confided to his diary on October 17. Bush began to ask about a daring air rescue of the 130 U.S. diplomats and embassy personnel under Iraqi guard in Kuwait City. Bush assumed that the Iraqis would fire on U.S. helicopters and that this could be the trigger for a massive American air attack. "I'm not sure where our country is. But if they saw a clear provocation, and I think that would include unwillingness to permit us to get our [embassy] people out of Kuwait, they would be supportive of knocking the hell out of this guy. We can do it from the air. Our military is waffling and vacillating in terms of what we can do on the ground." Curiously in this scenario, Bush appeared prepared to sacrifice the lives of some of the diplomats. Margaret Thatcher, with whom Bush shared this idea, reacted badly to it. Scowcroft, Cheney, and Baker were equally unenthusiastic.

On October 19 Baker and Powell met to discuss the latter's concerns about U.S. policy. Both men believed that U.S. policy was "drifting" and agreed to work together to push a tougher strategy of increasing diplomatic and political pressure on Saddam, which would involve beefing up the number of U.S. troops in the Gulf, to see whether Saddam or his regime would crack without the use of force. Baker worried not only about the erosion of support but also that the president was too eager to go to war now.

• • •

By the end of October the military planners had reluctantly drafted a two-corps plan, which would involve the deployment of over 400,000 U.S. troops. Rejecting Cheney's hobbyhorse of dropping troops into the Iraqi western desert and using the Baghdad–Amman road to threaten the capital, they proposed the left hook that Scowcroft had asked about. As a realistic ground war plan emerged, Powell showed that he was uncomfortable with it. When he offered it to the National Security Council on October 31, Powell exaggerated the number of troops and amount of matériel required to pull it off, in the hope that the plan would be rejected. But Bush wanted to preserve this option, and so he disarmed Powell by assuring him that the Pentagon would get "whatever it needed."

Bush had not yet given up on the provocation strategy. As it happened, in November it would be the United States' turn to hold the revolving presidency of the UN Security Council, and Bush wanted the State Department to draft a war resolution that set a January deadline for Iraq to leave Kuwait and included a right for the United States to "replenish" its embassies. The effort to send supplies into the embassies might draw Iraqi fire. The deadline was consistent with the Pentagon's assumption that it would be ready to launch a ground war three weeks after the last soldier disembarked at U.S. bases in Saudi Arabia. At the end of November the Security Council would pass Resolution 679, setting January 15 as the deadline by which Iraq had to leave Kuwait.

Bush also decided to change his public rhetoric to prepare the American people for the conflict that he thought was inevitable. Bush had always been a reluctant realist. It pained him that occasionally what was in U.S. interests was not always the same as unequivocally defending the Christian, moral precepts he had grown up with. The tough calls after Tiananmen and the Lithuania crisis lacked a moral clarity though they were strategically defensible. Saddam's action eliminated any moral confusion for Bush and permitted this emotional man to launch a full-throated call for unity in this war. In his statements and speeches Bush started to compare Saddam to Adolf Hitler.

For the pragmatists around Bush, the president finding his voice was a mixed blessing. By comparing Saddam to Hitler, calling him "Hitler revisited," the president was now effectively expanding U.S. and coalition war aims. This was intentional on Bush's part. "I think of the Iraqi babies," Bush confided in his diary, "and yet, I think of the evil that is this man. He has not only to be checked, but punished." His advisers and his coalition partners, however, had not signed on to regime change. What happened if Saddam pulled out of Kuwait or was compelled to leave, and somehow remained in power? Although all analysts, and every moderate Arab leader, were predicting that the regime would collapse with the adventure in Kuwait, Bush's advisers were wary of requiring Saddam's removal. In late October Scowcroft instructed his deputy Robert

Gates to travel with the president on a campaign swing for the 1990 midterm elections to cool the rhetoric a little.

. . .

With his own advisers divided and because of his concerns about the fragility of public unity, Bush decided on a risky two-track strategy. Over the objections of Scowcroft, Cheney, and many others, he would seek congressional support for Resolution 679 and its January 15 deadline, while issuing a dramatic invitation to Saddam to send an envoy to the White House with the request that he also accept a reciprocal mission from James Baker. This had the advantage of blunting growing domestic concerns that Bush was not serious about seeking the peaceful removal of Saddam's forces from Kuwait while also securing support for a possible war. But by opening the door to diplomacy, it also carried the risk that Saddam might actually cave in at no cost to himself. Bush did not want diplomacy to save Saddam.

Bush was not, however, in complete control of his administration. While on a six-day trip to South America in early December (the most extensive by a U.S. president to that region since Eisenhower in 1960), Bush learned that the State Department had unilaterally announced that it would vacate the U.S. embassy in Kuwait. The U.S. embassy was "open" but "temporarily not staffed," said State Department spokesperson Margaret D. Tutwiler on December 7. Bush had still not fully given up on the idea of using the embassy as part of a ploy to provoke Saddam to go to war. Baker, however, thought this idea too dangerous, and just as he had done a decade earlier, when he announced the end of Bush's presidential campaign, he acted unilaterally to protect his best friend from himself. Since Saddam had announced the previous day that all westerners remaining against their will in Kuwait and Iraq would receive exit visas, Baker saw no reason to risk the lives of U.S. diplomats in Kuwait City any longer.

Baker's maneuver may have killed off Bush's provocation fantasy, but it did not diminish the president's conviction that force was necessary to achieve U.S. aims in the Gulf. And Bush had a good idea how the decision to use that force would be made: "The more I talk to these delegations, I'm convinced that I'm going to have to make the decision [alone], and I'm going to have to take the heat. I'm going to have to share credit with Congress and the world if it works quickly, [with] acceptable loss of life—whatever that is—and a quick defeat for Saddam; but if it drags out, not only will I take the blame, but I will probably have impeachment hearings," he wrote just before Christmas. Still worried that the world did not respect his toughness, Bush wrote, "I know the consequences if we fail, and I know what will happen if we let the 15th slide by and we look wimpish, or unwilling to do what we must do."

Baker used his special access to Bush to make every last effort for a diplomatic settlement. He wanted to fly to Baghdad. Bush said no. "I'm inclined to slam the door and leave it closed because the guy's jerking us around," Bush told Baker on January 2, 1991, but he granted his insistent secretary of state a chance to meet the Iraqis in Geneva. Scowcroft thought this unnecessary but understood that the president did not want to look as if he had given up on a chance for a diplomatic settlement.

On January 12 the Gulf war resolutions came up for votes in both houses, just three days before the UN deadline. The bipartisan Michel-Solarz resolution in the House and the Dole-Warner resolution in the Senate supported the use of force to implement the UN resolutions. These resolutions passed 250–183 in the House and 52–47 in the Senate. Bush's domestic gamble had paid off. The country would be united behind him when he pulled the trigger.

· · ·

The war, now renamed Operation Desert Storm, began on January 17 with an air offensive. Although the air campaign did not destroy as many Iraqi tanks as had been hoped, it destroyed the morale in the frontline Iraqi troops in Kuwait. As the air war began, Bush clung to his long-held belief that Saddam would topple easily in the face of a U.S. attack. Indeed his greater concern was that this would not be a fair fight. "How do we keep from having overkill? Most people don't see that as a scenario because they are convinced it will be long and drawn out with numerous body bags on the US side. But I want to be sure we are not in there pounding people." Bush assumed that after the waves of air attack, Saddam would be overthrown by his own people, and then the question would be when and how to end the war. At the very least, in addition to a complete withdrawal from Kuwait, he wanted all Iraqi nuclear and biological weapons sites destroyed and the bulk of Iraq's Republican Guard units, the cream of Saddam's army, defanged.

The crisis then acquired its first unexpected element. As bombs started dropping on Baghdad, Saddam retaliated by ordering nineteen rocket strikes—from mobile Scud launchers—on Israel. These weapons caused few casualties and despite initial false reports did not carry nerve gas or chemical warheads. But the attacks tested the coalition as Israel announced publicly that it would retaliate. Since the beginning of the crisis, Saddam had tried to complicate the politics of the region by reminding Arab moderates that they hated Israel more than they hated him. An Israeli intervention in the war might force the eight Arab countries to split off from the grand coalition. The Bush administration worked hard, ultimately sending Deputy Secretary of State Lawrence Eagleburger to Tel Aviv and antiaircraft Patriot missiles to Israel to calm nerves.

From Moscow came a far less unexpected challenge. Gorbachev called Bush on the second day after the air war began and asked the president to consider suspending the air campaign. The Soviets had not wanted the air campaign to begin in the first place and had tried to talk Bush out of it. Bush had gone ahead with the air war, and now Bush explained why he could not suspend it, especially since Saddam had just attacked Israel. Bush thought of the errors that Lyndon Johnson had made in undertaking bombing pauses to negotiate with the North Vietnamese, only to see these initiatives exploited by Hanoi to regroup.

And the last challenge came from home. On January 29, as he was having his face powdered before his State of the Union address, Bush learned that James Baker had announced, in response to yet another Soviet effort to get Washington and Baghdad to resume negotiations, that if Saddam promised to withdraw there would be a cease-fire. Despite the makeup, the president was livid. The secretary of state later apologized to his longtime friend for speaking his preference rather than U.S. policy.

As the air war dragged on and the coalition exhausted its target lists and still the Iraqi people did not overthrow their tyrant, George Bush grew impatient to launch the ground phase of the battle plan. Yet Schwarzkopf's command in Riyadh was reluctant to get started. Bush's impatience grew with each day, magnified by a press that began to sense overkill in the air campaign. "The Press conference went well today, but I worry that they're chipping away, pounding, pounding away on the fact that civilians are being hurt and still support seems to be holding," he noted in his diary.

When Saddam announced on February 15, following a visit by a Soviet envoy to Baghdad, that he would accept UN Resolution 660, which called for a complete withdrawal of Iraqi forces from Kuwait, Bush confided that this was no longer enough. He wanted Saddam out. "My emotion is not one of elation. We've got some unfinished business. How do we solve it? How do we guarantee the future peace? I don't see how it will work with Saddam in power, and I am very, very wary." Bush then told Cheney and Baker to ignore Saddam's statement and press forward. Fortunately, when the full offer was publicized it contained so many conditions, including the rebuilding of Iraq and solving the Arab-Israeli question, that the administration paid no price in dismissing it altogether. Bush revealed some of his inner hopes with a few impromptu words added to a statement later in the day. He told the Iraqi people that if they took matters into their own hands, the bloodshed would end.

Meanwhile Bush steadied the Pentagon, which also hoped that Saddam's army would collapse without the start of a ground war. "It will be grisly," warned Powell. Playing on the president's political concerns, he added, "There will be pool reports of dead Americans." Bush then asked, "Do you prefer a negotiated settlement?" When Powell said yes, Bush let him know that Saddam had to be punished. "If they crack under force, it is better than withdrawal," he said.

Forty-five minutes before the deadline for the start of the ground war on February 24, Gorbachev called once again to ask for more time to get Saddam to back down. "These are the words of a friend," said Gorbachev. Bush said that time had run out. The coalition had amassed more than 800,000 troops, of which more than 500,000 were American, and Iraq had been given enough chances.

• • •

The ground war began with the invasion of Kuwait by the U.S. Marine Corps. The 85,000 marines deployed just south of the Kuwaiti border were given the mission to attack first so as to draw Iraq's best units down from the Tigris and Euphrates rivers into the path of the U.S., British, and French left hook. The flaw with the plan became clear within hours of the start of the land war. The Iraqi occupation army in Kuwait was nowhere near as strong as the coalition had assumed, and it collapsed in front of the marines. Despite satellite reconnaissance, signals intelligence (intercepted Iraqi messages), and information from informants, U.S. intelligence had not picked up that it was facing a shell of an army. Postwar assessments later concluded that the forty-two-division, 540,000-man Iraqi army of occupation had melted away to about 200,000 by the start of the land war, and many of those troops were prepared to give up. Those in the Iraqi army who might have wanted to fight were at a disadvantage because their leadership assumed that the Western forces could not fight in the open desert. The Iraqis projected their own limitations on the invaders. Lacking satellite-linked geostationary devices, the Iraqis restricted their movements to existing roads, and they expected coalition forces, despite their advanced technology, to do the same.

Seeing the amount of ground taken by the marines, Schwarzkopf ordered the bulk of the coalition forces to execute the left hook from the western desert a day earlier than planned. The U.S. army attacked, but its leadership, especially the commander of the pivotal VII Corps, was too cautious, refused to fight at night, and still acted as if it faced the best army in the third world.

Having rejected the Soviet suggestion that he avert a ground war at the eleventh hour by promising to withdraw from Kuwait, Saddam Hussein ordered a hasty general retreat from Kuwait on February 25 before the U.S. Army had even crossed into the country. With Iraqi forces streaming north, Schwarzkopf tried to accelerate his forces executing the left hook to trap as many of these forces as possible before they reached central Iraq.

The land war was proceeding as well as Bush had assumed but without the effect on Saddam's leadership. Almost alone among his advisers he had predicted that the Iraqi military would fold without many casualties. Only 147 Americans and 87 other members of the coalition armies died in combat. And now that Kuwait was effectively liberated, Bush faced a dilemma. The overkill that he had worried about was indeed starting to happen. He received reports—which later turned out to be exaggerated—of the destruction of columns of Iraqi forces along what was dubbed "the highway of death." Not only did Bush not want to be responsible for a massacre, but he understood that the coalition had united only on the objective of driving Saddam out of Kuwait. Beyond that, the thirty-three countries were not in agreement.

Bush thought he knew what needed to be done: "[Saddam is] getting clobbered and we're about to have him cut off at Basra . . . We must disarm the Republican Guard," he noted in his diary. Bush was confused as to how to end this war. And he even contemplated continuing it long enough, despite expected UN and coalition opposition, to achieve both of his goals. "It seems to me that we may get to a place where we have to choose between solidarity at the UN and ending this thing definitively," he wrote in his diary. "I am for the latter because our credibility is at stake. We don't want to have another draw, another Vietnam, a sloppy ending . . . We're not going to permit a sloppy ending where this guy emerges saving face."

No one on the Bush team, especially not the president, had expected that Saddam would still be standing as his Kuwaiti adventure collapsed around him. "Why do I not feel elated?" Bush asked his advisers, without expecting a response, as he received reports from the field. Saddam's army was leaving Kuwait, his forces were bloodied, and the U.S. military believed that all of his nuclear facilities had been destroyed. Yet the expected collapse of the regime had not happened.

On February 27, four days into the war, Bush resigned himself to the prospect that for the moment he would achieve his public war aim and nothing else. He could not see a way to justify continuing the Gulf War. Reports from the field as to how many of Saddam's Republican Guard units had been destroyed were confused, and it was not clear whether the pincers of the coalition attack north of Kuwait had reached a point where the "gate was closed," meaning that the Republican Guard units near the Iraqi-Kuwaiti border would be prevented from escaping deep inside Iraq. Nevertheless, Bush and the Gang of Eight decided without debate just after 6:00 P.M to end the war at midnight (Washington time), the one-hundred-hour point of the ground war, an arbitrary number that John Sununu thought had a nice ring to it. This happened without Bush's war council ever formally discussing using military means to achieve his second, private goal of driving Saddam completely from power. If there were any contingency plans for going to Baghdad, they had never seriously been considered. The Pentagon had not even formulated a plan for the occupation of the city. Having experienced the two-week delay in capturing Noriega in Panama, a country the United States knew much better than Iraq, the Bush administration did not even know whether a military campaign designed to find Saddam Hussein would succeed.

As Bush agreed to a cease-fire, his last hope for getting rid of Saddam was that the Iraqi army might still take matters into its own hands once the scale of the defeat sank in—the United States had destroyed twenty to thirty regular Iraqi divisions and four of Saddam's ten elite Republican Guard divisions. "Still no feeling of euphoria," Bush confided to his diary on February 28. "He's got to go . . . Obviously when the troops straggle home with no armor, beaten up, 50,000 casualties and maybe more dead, the people of Iraq will know." U.S. policy toward the defeated Iraqi military reflected this hope. Schwarzkopf was very respectful when he met with Iraqi generals at Safwan to discuss the terms of the cease-fire. When the Iraqi side asked to use helicopters to resupply their forces scattered around the country, the American commander agreed.

Within a few days the situation in Iraq collapsed. Hopeful that the Iraqi army would splinter, Shiite opponents of the regime led an uprising in the south that was joined by army deserters. On March 6 forces loyal to Saddam led a two-day counteroffensive that resulted in the deaths of 30,000 to 60,000 people. Meanwhile in the north, 50,000 Kurds started their own armed revolt. On March 27 the Iraqi army put down this revolt, killing 20,000 and creating a humanitarian crisis when 2 million Kurds fled from their homes. Although Bush had appealed to the Iraqi people to take their destiny into their own hands, it was not U.S. policy to support the dismantling of Iraq. As events spiraled out of control, the administration debated whether to do anything to help the Shiites or the Kurds. Pressure came from the British to join in a covert operation to assist the rebels, but Bush and his advisers agreed that America had no interest in seeing Iraq turn into a weak fragmented state like Lebanon. Iraq was needed to balance Iran in the Gulf. Bush therefore decided that he could do no more than provide humanitarian assistance for the Kurds. Operation Provide Comfort, which began in mid-April, ultimately provided food and shelter in UN-sanctioned camps for 400,000 refugees.

The world paid little attention to the final chapter of the Gulf War. The coalition had achieved the liberation of Kuwait, the goal for which it had been created. The U.S. military won its first major victory since World War II. The stain of Vietnam, Bush believed, was removed. Although Bush was disappointed that Saddam remained in power, this hardly diminished his pride at having led the country through a victorious war. "I felt the division in the country in the 60s and 70s," he noted. "I remember the agony and the ugliness, and now it's together." Privately, however, the administration began to consider covert ways of continuing the pressure on Saddam Hussein. It also established a no-fly zone in the north to protect the Kurds. Unknown to anyone at the time, the Iraqi dictator not only would remain a problem for a long time but would come to shape the historical destiny of a future, and different, Bush administration.

_____

6

The Collapse

George Bush had been one of the oldest men to be elected president. But this was not how Americans thought of him, especially since Ronald Reagan had been truly elderly when he left office. In better shape than most men his age, blessed with boyish looks, a full head of hair, and deep wells of energy, Bush seemed at least a decade younger than his years. "This President relaxes by wearing the others out," noted Maureen Dowd of the *New York Times*. Bush's verbal and physical tics might have come off a bit freakish, deepening the sense that he was awkward, but they did not make him seem old.

In the spring of 1991, however, the health of the nearly sixty-seven-year-old president became an issue for the first time. While jogging at Camp David on the morning of May 4, he became short of breath and had to stop. Bush had been complaining of fatigue for six weeks; he had lost fifteen pounds, and his secretary, Patty Presock, had noticed a change in his handwriting. But until that morning no one knew what the problem might be. After giving him some tests, the president's doctors determined that he had a fibrillation, or irregular heartbeat. Days later it became clear that he was suffering from Graves' disease, which caused an overactive thyroid that had to be treated by radiation and replacement with hormonal supplements. (In a remarkable coincidence, Barbara Bush had already been diagnosed with this same rare disease in 1989.) "Oh no," he thought as he sat in the Camp David clinic on the day of the jogging incident, "here comes a bunch of Democrats charging out of the woodwork to run."

The president, who could hardly have seemed more popular, had allowed himself to dream of reelection by acclamation in 1992. Bathed in a sea of small American flags carried by every member of the audience, Bush had spoken to a joint session of Congress on March 6 to celebrate the end of the Gulf War. That month his presidential approval rating had hit 89 percent, higher than it had ever been for Ronald Reagan. By May it had dropped some but was still at the remarkable level of 75 percent. Although Election Day was still eighteen months off, Bush's reelection seemed as sure a thing as one could expect in American politics. Russell Baker, the venerable *New York Times* columnist, said that George Bush had gained "a popularity and stature almost inconceivable for any president in his third year in office." Faced with these long odds, many of the heavy hitters in the Democratic Party—Governor Mario Cuomo of New York, Senator Al Gore of Tennessee, and House majority leader Richard Gephardt of Missouri—would decide not to run.

What neither the leading Democrats nor those around Bush in the GOP appreciated at the time was that the support for the president was as shallow as it was wide. The end of the Cold War had unleashed pent-up energies at home just as it had abroad. To some extent, the baby boomers were shifting national priorities, as they had done since the late 1960s. The eldest members of this group, born in the years following World War II, were hitting middle age in the early 1990s. In the late 1960s many of them had protested Vietnam and their parents' values. Now they were unsettled by the appearance of a lowered standard of living and the reality of the cost of their own kids' education. Besides the usual cultural and psychological consequences of hitting middle age, this generation was being bombarded with concerns that their parents had never experienced. The vast majority of the World War II generation was still enjoying its so-called golden years, financed by robust retirement packages and pensions that allowed many to retire by age sixty-five with a large percentage of their salaries. In addition, many companies provided additional medical coverage, and among those who had worked for themselves or had been in smaller companies, so many were World War II and Korean War veterans that they could rely on the Veterans Administration hospital system. By the late 1980s the Vietnam/Flower Power generation was coming to realize that it would not have these protections. Their children were going to deteriorating schools. If they wanted the American dream, many believed they would have to move farther from their place of work. Since those who left the cities tended to be white, as the average commute to work got longer the national racial divide deepened. Meanwhile, the cost of college had jumped between 1980 and 1990, outpacing the rate of inflation. Finally, the end of the Cold War and the demobilization of a large portion of the defense industry and the reduction in the size of the U.S. military seemed to portend much higher rates of unemployment in the future.

But the baby boomers were not the only source of instability in the American body politic or of Bush's political vulnerability. The domestic chaos of the late 1960s and the early 1970s, combined with the failures of the Nixon administration and the consequences of Vietnam, inspired sharply divergent interpretations of what had gone wrong. Ronald Reagan had developed a personal connection with those who believed that both Washington and the Left had let the country down. Most energized were a bloc of social conservatives, who viewed federal efforts to uphold the Constitution's separation of church and state, to defend a woman's right to choose, to protect flag burning as free speech, to institute sex education in school as part of an elitist plot to banish God and orthodox morality from modern society. Bush's restrained personal piety and his previous history of being more liberal on abortion and women's rights made him suspect among the growing number of religious conservatives. And among these voters, Bush's actions as a good-government Republican did not outweigh his weaknesses as a cultural conservative.

Worse for Bush, his fiscal prudence was not attracting centrists, either. A close look at Bush's approval numbers shows that the Gulf War—when foreign policy seemed to matter again—had given an artificial bounce to what had been a steady erosion of the president's popular support since the end of his first year in office. By the end of 1990, despite general approval for Bush's efforts in the Middle East, only 34 percent of those polled gave him a passing grade at home. Bush's problem was that while he was held responsible for the financial mess left by Reagan, no one seemed to give him credit for trying to fix it.

There were few sweeteners for the bitter medicine of the S&L bailout and the 1990 budget agreement. Acid rain was the third negative domestic legacy of the Reagan administration that Bush, who was far more committed to conservation and the environment than Reagan, tackled early on in his term. The 1990 Clean Air Amendments introduced an innovative system to harness market incentives to force companies to lower their emissions of sulfur dioxide, the principal cause of acid rain in North America. The administration also showed a concern about global warming. In 1992 it would join more than 150 other countries in signing the UN Framework Convention on Climate Change, or Rio Treaty, which set voluntary guideposts for the reduction of greenhouse emissions. Otherwise Bush was not that active on domestic issues. Despite having campaigned as "the education president," and having described education as "our most enduring legacy," he was not able to make any significant progress on that challenging issue. Besides the Clean Air Amendments, Bush's major legislative achievements, the Americans with Disabilities Act and the Civil Rights Act of 1991, reflected congressional priorities more than his own. These were significant pieces of legislation, and the ADA empowered the disabled, including those with AIDS, by lowering barriers, real and symbolic, to full participation in American society. But they garnered little public support for George Bush.

On the Supreme Court, where presidents often leave their most lasting mark, George Bush also managed to satisfy very few. He filled his first vacancy, following the retirement of the influential liberal justice William Brennan in the summer of 1990, with a little-known judge from New Hampshire named David Souter, who turned out to be far less conservative than most of his backers assumed, especially Chief of Staff Sununu, his principal advocate in the White House. As Souter began to compile an impressive record as a sober member of what until the 1980s would have been seen as the center of the Court, some in the Bush White House would blame him for having hidden his views in an attempt to get on the Court. Bush's second appointment, to replace the retiring civil rights pioneer Thurgood Marshall in 1991, was controversial from the start. Clarence Thomas was a darling of the Reagan Right. An energetic conservative from a poverty-stricken background, he seemed to answer the Republican Party's hope to promote and recruit like-minded African Americans. With the appearance of Anita Hill, a law professor and former assistant to Clarence Thomas at both the U.S. Department of Education and the Equal Employment Opportunity Commission, Thomas's Senate confirmation hearings soon descended into a soap opera. No one who participated in the Thomas hearings came off well. By the end, the nation had been exposed to discussions of sexual harassment, pornographic videos, and pubic hair left on a Coke can. Both parties in Congress and the Bush White House exhibited scars from the doomed fight in the second Reagan term over the nomination of Judge Robert Bork to the Court, which had happened only four years earlier. Neither party wished to give up; ultimately there proved to be not enough evidence to deny the president his choice, even if there was no consensus as to whether Thomas was fit for the job. In October 1991 the U.S. Senate narrowly confirmed Thomas, 52–48.

· · ·

In 1991, as doctors sought to stabilize Bush's thyroid problem, the Soviet Union entered a terminal crisis. The economy was in freefall. With galloping inflation and a severe reduction in imports, the Soviet Union faced the possibility of a 25 percent decrease in gross domestic product. In late March 1991 more than 100,000 people took to the streets of Moscow in an unprecedented display of popular activism to protest against Gorbachev and the dramatic increases in the cost of living. Nationalists and hard-line conservatives alike were eager to take advantage of Gorbachev's increasing weakness. In April the Supreme Soviet of the Russian Federation passed a law permitting the election of a Russian president, opening the door to Boris N. Yeltsin to become the first elected leader in Russian history in June. Meanwhile opponents of market reforms and Gorbachev's increasingly frantic effort to decentralize the Soviet Union to accommodate rising nationalist tensions called for a special meeting of the Central Committee of the Soviet Communist Party. On April 24, 1991, Gorbachev threatened to resign to shore up his position in the party's inner circle, the Politburo.

Although it was U.S. policy to support Gorbachev, there was debate within the Bush administration over what lengths to take to prop him up. From the hard Right, Dick Cheney argued that it was time to embrace the nationalists and separatists. If Yeltsin in Russia and Leonid Kravchuk in Ukraine got their way, the Soviet Union would implode and whatever was left of the Cold War would go with it. From James Baker and the State Department, the president received the opposite advice. In late May the U.S. embassy in Moscow sent a pointed request that Bush do more to help Gorbachev. Taking advantage of a meeting with former British prime minister Margaret Thatcher, who believed that "only American leadership" could shore up Gorbachev and perestroika, U.S. ambassador Jack Matlock wrote, "I think that Mrs. Thatcher is right. One can find many excuses, indeed reasons, for doing nothing . . . [b]ut we should organize a very substantial program to support and help guide the reform effort here."

Seeking a middle ground, Bush chose to provide symbolic support to Gorbachev without making any major financial investments in the bizarre mixed economy that the Soviet Union was slapping together. The Soviets were invited to join the World Bank and the International Monetary Fund, but Bush did not support a massive infusion of financial support to create a functional Soviet economy. Meanwhile, Bush sought to exploit Soviet weakness. In July 1991 Bush came to Moscow for what would turn out to be the last U.S.-Soviet summit. Earlier Bush had sent the Conventional Forces in Europe (CFE) Treaty to the Senate for ratification. Although the landmark agreement—limiting NATO, Soviet, and former Warsaw Pact conventional forces in Europe—had been signed in November 1990, foot-dragging by hard-liners in the Soviet military had caused Washington to suspend ratification. Prior to Bush's arrival Gorbachev had overruled the conservatives in the military, permitting Bush to lift the hold, and the Kremlin had equally good news on the issue of emigration and nuclear arms reductions. Soviet citizens could now emigrate at will, removing a major political hurdle to broadening trade between the United States and the Soviet Union. The START Treaty, which the Soviets now accepted, would reduce the U.S. strategic arsenal by 25 percent and the Soviet arsenal by 35 percent, bringing the nuclear balance back to what it had been before 1982.

Events had spun so far out of Gorbachev's control that these achievements in behalf of world peace offered no discernible political advantage for him. On June 12 Boris Yeltsin was elected president of Russia with 57 percent of the popular vote. For the first time Moscow and Leningrad (whose citizens also voted to change its name back to St. Petersburg) also got democratically elected mayors. Meanwhile, a proposed Union Treaty, which was due to be signed by the republics on August 20, would pass new power to them and remove the words *Soviet* and *Socialist* from the name of the country. This was all too much for Moscow's remaining hard-liners. On August 19, while Gorbachev was on holiday, a conspiracy of six high-level Kremlin officials mounted a coup, declaring a six-month state of emergency and the transfer of presidential powers from Gorbachev to his deputy Gennady Yanayev.

Bush bungled his initial response to the long-feared coup. On the advice of Brent Scowcroft, he issued a statement that not only did not condemn the coup (which he merely called extraconstitutional) but implied that the Gorbachev era was over and that the United States was resigned to having to deal with the junta. For months the president had worried that perhaps he was not doing enough rhetorically to help his friend Gorbachev. Now, when that help was needed the most, Bush was a victim of his own prudence.

The coup, however, collapsed without needing a push from the West. Boris Yeltsin rallied his supporters in front of the Russian parliament in Moscow and challenged the Kremlin's new leaders to come after him. In an image that captured his defiance, Yeltsin climbed atop a tank and waved his fist at the coup plotters. When the Soviet army and the KGB refused orders to attack Yeltsin, the coup was over. Drunk, disillusioned, and afraid, the conservative hard-liners in the Kremlin gave up on August 22 and asked Gorbachev for forgiveness. He responded by throwing them in jail.

Gorbachev's political authority dissolved along with the coup. He returned to Moscow a shadow of his former self. Several prominent Soviet citizens had used the coup as an excuse to finally leave the Communist Party. Gorbachev himself contemplated doing the same, but without it he would have had no political base at all. The sole elected leader in Russia, Boris Yeltsin, seized on Gorbachev's weakness to dismantle the Communist Party in Russia. Meanwhile many of the former Soviet republics declared their independence.

By year's end Gorbachev himself announced that the Union of Soviet Socialist Republics would itself be dissolved. For the first time,
the United States was the world's lone superpower.

. . .

George Bush chose not to manage the breakup of Yugoslavia as
actively as he had events in eastern Europe and the former Soviet
Union. He considered this crumbling multiethnic state to be a
regional European dispute, and its unity was not a vital interest
to the United States. The Bush administration's main concern was
that the Europeans ensure that the conflict not spread beyond Yugoslavia's borders. The nationalist wave sweeping eastern Europe and
the former Soviet Union had magnified tensions that had started
building after the death of Yugoslavia's longtime Communist leader,
Josip Broz Tito, in 1980. In the summer of 1991, after Slovenia and
Croatia unilaterally declared their independence, a brief war erupted
between Slovenia and the Serbian-controlled Yugoslav army. A
longer struggle, involving Croatian Serbs with the assistance of the
Yugoslav government, also started in Croatia. Hopeful to achieve
peace in Croatia and concerned about the fate of the other non-
Serbian republics of Yugoslavia—Macedonia, Bosnia-Herzegovina,
Montenegro—the Bush administration maintained a policy of non-
recognition, advising its European allies to do the same while asking them to take the lead in resolving the widening conflict. The
European Community, however, worked by unanimity, and whereas
Italy and Germany tended to support Slovenia and Croatia, France
and Great Britain tilted toward Serbia. The effect was near paralysis.

In August 1991 Bush used a speech in Kiev to send a message
over the heads of his Ukrainian audience to the Yugoslavs to slow
the disintegration of their state, so that political will and diplomacy, not violence, would dictate the outcome. "Freedom is not the
same as independence," said Bush. "Americans will not support
those who seek independence in order to replace a far-off tyranny

with a local despotism." Derided at home as the "Chicken Kiev" speech, because it implied a lack of support for Ukrainian self-determination, the speech captured Bush's belief that national self-determination alone was not a guarantee that the successor states of any empire would be liberal democracies.

As Washington had feared, centrifugal forces increased dramatically in the region when Germany recognized Slovenia and Croatia in December 1991 and the European Community followed suit a month later. Although a UN- and EC-sponsored plan did reduce the violence in Croatia in January 1992, the war soon spread to Bosnia, after it declared its own independence in April. The Serbs laid siege to Sarajevo, the Bosnian capital, and by May had the city completely blockaded. Again, the U.S. government—which recognized Slovenia, Croatia, and Bosnia in late April—wanted the Europeans to take care of the situation. And again, the Europeans proved largely ineffectual. In June 1992 Bush authorized the use of U.S. transport planes to deliver relief to the besieged city, where ultimately over 10,000 would die, but only if there was a cease-fire. Although James Baker wanted to use force to get relief to the people of Sarajevo, the president wanted to avoid any military intervention in Bosnia. The violence around Sarajevo would last another three years.

. . .

George Bush entered the reelection year of 1992 without an enemy abroad but with many at home. Had he announced that he was not seeking reelection, Bush would instantly have been remembered as the statesman who had managed the Cold War to a soft landing while setting the new rules of the road for petty tyrants like Saddam Hussein. Instead, he decided that he wanted a second term. George Washington deserves credit for voluntarily leaving office at a time when a grateful nation would have allowed him to be commander in chief for life, but he also left the legacy of a second term. Most presidents, with the notable exception of James K. Polk (who pledged not to seek a second term when he ran for the office in 1844), have sought reelection as a kind of redemption for the criticisms of their first term and to seal their legacy as a good president.

By early 1992 it was clear to most observers that Bush faced an uphill reelection battle. The decisions of the first two years—especially the S&L bailout—had had a negative impact on the economy. The country was in a recession, which, though ultimately short-lived, hit hardest the segment of society, white-collar workers, where Bush most needed support to have any hope of reelection. In June 1991 the unemployment rate hit 6.9 percent, the highest in nine years. The political effect on Bush was magnified because in the wake of the 1990 budget deal, he lacked a loyal conservative base. Clayton Yeutter, who became chairman of the Republican National Committee in 1991, later asserted that from June 1990, "Bush assumed a defensive posture politically and stayed there for the remainder of his presidency." The Right assailed him for betraying Reagan by raising taxes, and the Left attacked him for being a Republican. The center, his natural constituency, didn't really know him and thought he had sold his soul to the conservatives anyway.

Bush became the object of increasing public scorn. An unfortunate incident in Japan in January, when he took ill and vomited on the Japanese prime minister during a state dinner in Tokyo, caused more ridicule than concern. In this noxious political environment press reports of Bush being out of touch with ordinary Americans seemed to ring true. Bush was widely reported to have been mystified by scanners at a supermarket checkout counter—although the incident was later shown to have been a misunderstanding.

Although burdened by some bad luck and bad press, Bush made matters worse by reacting ineptly to his image problems. Curiously, despite having taken some of the hardest decisions a president had made in a generation, he opted not to launch his reelection bid on the back of his decisiveness in Europe, in the Gulf, and on the budget. Instead, Bush announced that he felt raising taxes had been a mistake, and later he agreed with his advisers to shelve plans for commercials that trumpeted his achievements in war. The surprise loss of former attorney general Richard Thornburgh in a special election in Pennsylvania for the U.S. Senate in 1991 had convinced Republican strategists that foreign policy success could not outweigh public concerns about the economy. A vacuum had opened in U.S. politics, and across the political spectrum there was a hunger for somebody new to step forward.

. . .

The first challenge to George Bush came from within his own party. The Gingrich rebellion had emboldened the right wing, leading to an insurgent presidential campaign by the political commentator and former Nixon speechwriter Patrick Buchanan, who attempted to rally populist conservatives against Bush. Besides attacking the 1990 budget deal, Buchanan assailed Bush for his commitment to free trade, especially the North American Free Trade Agreement with Canada and Mexico, which was on its way to the Senate for ratification. Buchanan was a nativist and a protectionist whose campaign echoed the insurgency of Alabama's George Wallace in 1968 and 1972. With little money, Buchanan nevertheless ran a strong campaign among Republican activists and received 37 percent of the vote in the New Hampshire primary in February. Though Buchanan's campaign soon ran out of steam, his success was a wake-up call to Bush that he would have to fight hard to ensure that the Reaganite base came out to vote for him in November.

Bush also had some concerns about the presumptive Democratic nominee, the young governor of Arkansas, Bill Clinton. Clinton was a masterful politician whose talents seemed even bigger as one learned about his manifest flaws. Clinton seemed a man of huge appetites and very little self-control. Evidence of infidelity, which had killed the campaign of another Democratic front-runner, Senator Gary Hart, in the 1988 cycle, hardly made a dent in Clinton's popularity after he and his wife, Hillary, sat for a joint interview aired on the television news magazine *60 Minutes* after the Super Bowl.

Bush thought he could beat Clinton. As he told the speechwriter Peggy Noonan, "He's better at facts-figures than I am. I'm better at life." It would take a psychologist to understand how much of George Bush's underestimation of Bill Clinton was a reflection of his troubled relationship with his eldest son, George W. Bush, who was the same age as the Arkansas governor. Both Clinton and George W. had found a way to avoid military service in Vietnam. Both had shown personal recklessness, though Clinton's came in the bedroom whereas that of Bush's son came in the barroom. The comparisons, however, stopped there. Clinton had been a Rhodes Scholar and a successful governor, whereas George W. had taken a long time to find his way. Yet it is also possible that the elder Bush underestimated Clinton simply because he was so young. Clinton would be the first baby boomer nominated for the presidency, while George Bush seemed to be the last of the World War II generation.

Although Bush appeared sluggish and less interested in the campaign, he made some moves in the spring of 1992 to improve his team. "These are weird and ugly political times," he told Jack Welch, the celebrated CEO of General Electric. Bush brought Noonan back in April. Noonan had gained fame, and some resentment, as the writer behind some of Reagan's best lines as president. And Bush also asked George W. to devote himself full-time as a consultant. Despite these changes, the Bush team still lacked two key players from 1988. Lee Atwater, the consultant responsible for the divisive tactics that had tainted Bush among moderates, had died of cancer in 1991. Bush's abrasive chief of staff, John Sununu, had been hounded from office several months later, when reports surfaced that he had used government cars and planes for his own private benefit. The last key member missing from the 1988 team was James Baker himself. Baker loved being secretary of state and in 1992 was moving rapidly to establish a diplomatic process to improve Arab-Israeli relations. He did not want to return to the grubby business of domestic politicking.

But 1992 was no ordinary political year, and the main reason for this was the entry of a diminutive Texas businessman named H. Ross Perot into the presidential race.

Ross Perot and George Bush had known each other for thirty years, and until the 1980s they had been on reasonably good terms. The turning point between them had come when Ronald Reagan had asked his vice president to manage the controversy over whether the Vietnamese were still holding any American prisoners of war (POWs) or men missing in action (MIAs). The Reagan administration assumed that there were no Americans still living in Vietnam against their will, but a large number of Americans believed otherwise. Indeed, some were convinced that the U.S. government maintained, for one reason or another, a conspiracy of silence to deny credible intelligence that POWs and MIAs were still being held in Southeast Asia. Perot was the most energetic and effective of those arguing that Washington had to do more to close this chapter of the Vietnam War. In 1987 Reagan had asked Bush to tell Perot that his administration would not support appointing him a special adviser on the POW problem. Bush was also asked to tell Perot that his trips to Vietnam were hurting the official visits by General John Vessey, the former chairman of the Joint Chiefs of Staff, who was leading an official POW/MIA probe. Perot refused to take no for an answer, and it was Bush, the messenger, who got hurt. "I'm disappointed in him," Bush wrote in his diary in May 1987. "I've always had him on a high plane, high regard; but, he has acted badly and has not kept his word. For example, he said he would not go to Vietnam unless he saw live prisoners. He said that over and over again, and then he went . . . There's no question about his intention, but he is just too much."

In 1992 the Perot presidential campaign was a creation of the media. In February he appeared on a radio station in Tennessee at the request of some local backers who had been pressuring him for months to think about running for president. In response to a question about his presidential ambitions, Perot told the caller that he would consider running if volunteers put his name on every state ballot. A few weeks later he repeated the pledge on the popular CNN talk show *Larry King Live*. Reflecting the general dissatisfaction with Bush, calls started coming in to Perot's businesses, and by the end of March he had hired the Home Shopping Network, which specialized in impulse shopping by telephone, to supervise twelve hundred separate phone lines.

Around this time, seasoned Republican leaders started paying attention. On March 31 former senators Howard Baker of Tennessee and James McClure of Idaho made a point over lunch with Bush to express their concern about Perot. Bush, who thought Perot a crank, assured them that within three months Perot would have self-destructed and his political movement along with him. "Perot will be defined," claimed Bush, "seen as a weirdo, and we shouldn't be concerned with him." They said, "We hope you're right but we don't agree with you." Baker and McClure said that "the move for change is so much outside, that outsiders are in and insiders are out; and that Perot can take his money and parlay himself into victory or into a serious threat."

As the spring wore on, and it became clear that Perot was in the race, Bush's antagonism toward Perot grew stronger. After a conversation with Bush in mid-June, Richard Nixon (who had briefly turned on the Bush administration a few months earlier for not being aggressive enough in supporting Boris Yeltsin and the new Russia) noted that "his criticisms could only be described as vitriolic." At the same time Bush continued to believe that Perot, whom he described as "erratic" and "dictatorial," would self-destruct. He also assumed that Perot had the support only of "the extremists from Birchers to ultra-liberals." "What concerns me is that he still may not realize how serious the Perot challenge is," Nixon noted for the record.

Events in July 1992 initially seemed to prove Bush right. The Perot campaign seemed to collapse. Charging that Bush was trying to undermine his campaign and, in a weird aside, attack his family and sabotage his daughter's wedding, Perot left the race. Curiously, Bush then asked Perot for his support, arguing that the two men had more in common ideologically than Perot and Clinton. But though he had left the campaign—temporarily, as it turned out— Perot's personal dislike of Bush remained and he said no.

Perot's disappearance did not help Bush. After the Democratic convention in July, Bush's approval rating dropped to 29 percent. Only Harry Truman during the impasse of the Korean War (23 percent), Richard Nixon in the Watergate year of 1974 (24 percent), and Jimmy Carter in 1979 (28 percent) had been more unpopular. Bush, however, was the first president to have ever suffered so swift an erosion of support. Nixon had seen his support crater after the 1972 election, but he had never been as popular as Bush had been at the end of the Gulf War. Bush, who had lived through Watergate, could not understand why he was experiencing a similar collapse in political support.

None of his predecessors had ever recovered from such a fall in public approval. Truman decided not to run again in 1952, Nixon had resigned, and Carter had been beaten by Reagan. According to the Gallup organization, no president since Truman in 1948 had ever been reelected with an approval rating under 50 percent in an election year. Although Bush refused to believe this would happen, in the late summer of 1992 professionals began a deathwatch over his campaign.

In August the Bush campaign was desperate for better management. The unemployment rate had actually started to fall—after peaking at 7.8 percent in June—but it was still at 7.6 percent, and while there were other signs that the economy was picking up the recovery was painfully slow. Bush was having a hard time selling the line that the recession was over. The president pleaded with his old friend James Baker to return to active politics, and the secretary of state stepped down to return to the White House as chief of staff, a post he had last held for Reagan in 1985. Before leaving Foggy Bottom, Baker managed the regional peace conference in Madrid that Bush had promised Gorbachev as a coalition-building sweetener in 1990. The Middle East had not looked as calm since well before the Six-Day War of 1967. Not only were Arabs and Israelis talking, but the Palestine Liberation Organization had dropped its insistence that the state of Israel be destroyed. Meanwhile there was not a single American hostage remaining in the Arab world. Ironically, when Saddam Hussein invaded Kuwait he had released the Al-Sabah government's political prisoners, among whom were members of a Shiite extremist group that had tried to blow up the American and French embassies in 1983. It had been their release that Hezbollah had sought in taking American hostages in Lebanon. Once these extremists were released, Hezbollah's interest in holding Americans captive disappeared. By early 1992 all of the hostages were home. Only in Iraq itself could the region be described as less secure. Saddam crushed a serious coup attempt in June 1992, then sent forces south to root out guerrillas. In response, in August, the United States, France, and the United Kingdom established a second no-fly zone over the lower third of the country.

At the Republican National Convention in Houston, Bush's operatives worked hard to energize the party's restive conservatives. Pat Buchanan was given a prime-time speaking role, and he returned the compliment by sending a shrill, bigoted message that was at odds with Bush's promise to work toward a kinder, gentler nation. Despite efforts by James Baker and others to replace Dan Quayle on the ticket, the still politically damaged vice president remained as a symbol of Bush's commitment to young Reaganites.

As Bush attempted to revive his campaign after the Republican convention, Hurricane Andrew, a category five storm, devastated the southern coast of Florida and south-central Louisiana and raised additional questions about the competence of his administration. Although Bush wasted no time in declaring a state of emergency when the hurricane hit south of Miami on August 24, it took too many days for the U.S. government to respond adequately. The storm killed twenty-three people and caused an unprecedented amount of damage to homes and businesses, leaving many Floridians vulnerable. In large measure the problem was that policymakers lacked good information. Although his son Jeb was living in Miami, Bush did not know the extent of the devastation caused by Andrew for days. As of August 26 the Federal Emergency Management Agency was reporting to the White House that only 2,000 mobile homes had been destroyed and between 900 and 1,600 homes and apartments were left uninhabitable in Florida, which had suffered the brunt of the storm. In fact, so many dwellings had been destroyed that 189,000 people were homeless and lacked water and basic foodstuffs. Meanwhile, Florida state officials were equally surprised by the extent of the emergency. Some in the White House, who recalled the administration's equally slow response to the massive rioting in Los Angeles in April—sparked by the acquittal of three of four police officers charged with beating Rodney King, an African American motorist—pushed for Bush to name a "czar" to coordinate the federal response to this latest tragedy. Bush agreed, and he designated Secretary of Transportation Andrew Card to fill this role.

The handling of the situation started to improve when Card arrived at the scene on August 26. Card advocated the deployment of U.S. troops and pushed Florida governor Lawton Chiles to issue a formal request the next day for federal intervention, which was required under the law. On August 28 mobile kitchen trailers were flown in, and the first of 28,500 U.S. troops started arriving in southern Florida. On September 1 Bush and Secretary of Defense Cheney visited the area, where the Pentagon was building a tent city, and the following day an additional one million meals-ready-to-eat arrived to feed the homeless. With estimates of $45 billion in damage, Andrew exceeded the cost of any previous natural disaster in U.S. history.

Bush's political situation worsened further when Ross Perot returned to the race in October. The ever-mercurial Perot drew from the bases of both political parties, but he had a greater purchase on probable Republican voters because of his economic conservatism and outspoken support for the U.S. military. In the last Gallup poll before Perot rejoined the race, Clinton polled 50 percent and Bush 40 percent. In the next poll in early October, Clinton had 49 percent, Bush 34 percent, and Perot 10 percent. Three televised debates followed, in which Clinton and Perot both outshone Bush, who at one point was seen looking impatiently at his watch and generally failed to connect with voters concerned about the economy.

As his political career unraveled, Bush became oddly unrealistic. He told people that he expected a come-from-behind win. White House counsel C. Boyden Gray, a longtime friend, later recalled, "George Bush makes comebacks. That is the way he plays tennis, baseball and horseshoes." Perhaps Bush believed that there would be some helpful revelations about Clinton. State Department officials had launched an urgent search of the Democratic nominee's passport files, looking for damaging information regarding his student trip to Moscow in 1969. Nothing was found.

When the Iran-Contra independent counsel Lawrence Walsh announced the indictment of Caspar Weinberger on the final weekend of the campaign, however, Bush believed that his last chance at a comeback had been thwarted. Although the election was already lost, Bush had grown so bitter about how he was being treated by the press and, perhaps, by the fates that he stubbornly believed this indictment—whose timing may or may not have been politically motivated—had cost him the election. What the indictment did do, however, was raise those old questions of what Bush as vice president had known about Reagan's foreign policy mess. Excerpts from Weinberger's diary, which were included in the indictment, contradicted Bush's 1987 assertion that he had been "out of the loop."

Bush's defeat in November was complete and personal. The final tally was 43 percent for Clinton, 37 percent for Bush, and 19 percent for Perot—which meant that 63 percent voted against Bush. And though 13 million more votes were cast in 1992 than in 1988, the president actually received 9 million fewer votes. This was repudiation on a par with that experienced by Barry Goldwater in 1964 and George McGovern in 1972. And one had to reach back eighty years to see as great a collapse of national support for an incumbent president running for reelection. Ironically, Bush was sharing the fate of William Howard Taft, the previous Yale man in the White House, who had lost to Woodrow Wilson in 1912 in part because of a third-party challenge from Theodore Roosevelt. In 1992, however, the Republican Party did not suffer as much as its standard-bearer did. Indeed, while remaining in the minority in both houses of Congress, the GOP actually picked up nine seats in the House while holding its seats in the Senate.

With the end of the Cold War, the basic contours of American presidential politics were changing. Since 1940, with the exceptions of the elections of Harry S. Truman in 1948 and Jimmy Carter in 1976, foreign policy had figured prominently in every presidential horse race. Presidents might not be elected on the basis of their foreign policy platforms, but if they did not seem credible in standing up to the Nazis or later the Soviets, they could not come close to winning. In 1992, with the Soviet Union gone, the American people judged leadership by a different standard, summarized by a poster in the war room of the Clinton campaign: "It's the economy, stupid." Lacking a unified party and unable to translate foreign successes into personal popularity and public confidence at home, George Bush learned he had failed that test.

7

Paterfamilias

A week after the election, George and Barbara Bush made an impromptu late-night visit to the Vietnam Veterans Memorial. Maya Lin's huge *V*, which slices into the Mall in front of the Lincoln Memorial, is a somber symbol of a war that America lost. On its black granite face are carved the names of those who died in Vietnam. Just before midnight the president and the first lady read a few of them aloud. Veterans were marking the tenth anniversary of the unveiling of the memorial by sponsoring a daylong reading of the 58,137 names. The president was not expected to be there, but on an impulse George Bush had decided to participate. He had just come from a tear-filled farewell dinner with the Senate leadership at Union Station and was taking a lonely stroll on the South Lawn of the White House when the idea came to him. Barbara had already gone to bed, but he woke her up and asked the Secret Service whether a last-minute visit to the Mall could be arranged. Bush did not want to attract any attention lest anybody think he was trying to make some kind of statement about the fact that Bill Clinton had avoided service in that war. The campaign was over. The president had more personal reasons for going.

George Bush was hurting inside. He had been repudiated at the polls. He had expected to pull it off in the end, but the country had told him that his services were no longer required. And his mother was dying. For this very competitive, sensitive man these reversals produced an oppressive sense of defeat. "I will always regret not finishing the course," he wrote his brother Jonathan that November. "I recall the Kenyan runner in the Olympics who limped across the finish line 45 minutes behind the leaders. He was hurting bad. 'My country didn't send me all the way to start the race. They sent me here to finish it.' I didn't finish the course, and I will always regret that."

The visit to the granite *V* was a welcome reminder of his two proudest achievements: service as a very young man in World War II and his role as commander in chief in prosecuting two wars that helped the country overcome the burden of Vietnam. When asked as president what he wanted on his gravestone, Bush sketched a simple marker emblazoned with a cross and his serviceman's identification number on one side and "He loved Barbara very much" on the other. The twenty or so veterans at the memorial who were reading names with him and Barbara that night had not been allowed by their generation to have this much pride in their own military service. But the American people were now treating Gulf War veterans as heroes and seemed proud of their military again. Despite some political posturing, the U.S. Congress had also shown its solidarity. Not bad for a man whom some continued to call a wimp.

Less than two weeks after the visit to the Vietnam Memorial, Bush flew to Greenwich, Connecticut, with his daughter Dorothy ("Doro") to be by his mother's side in her last moments. A strict disciplinarian, she had established rules that still guided her son's life: "Don't walk ahead," "Don't use *I*," "Don't be a braggadocio," "How did the TEAM do?" They were as important in shaping the president that Bush became as his father's idea of "service." And now Bush was losing her along with the job he had sought his entire adult life. "Doro and I sat next to her bed sobbing," he confided that night. "Her little frayed Bible, her old one was there, and I looked in it and

there were some notes that I had written her from Andover."
Dorothy Walker Bush, age ninety-one, died later that day.

George Bush gave up trying to hide his feelings in those difficult
weeks. A rumor went around the White House that he was thinking of resigning before January 20. It wasn't true, but the dejection
was real. To perk up his staff and lay to rest the rumors, he invited
to the White House Dana Carvey, a comedian who had achieved
fame impersonating Bush's nasally halting cadence on the popular
television show *Saturday Night Live.* Without letting the staff in on
the surprise, he asked Carvey to appear as him at the start of a
Christmas party.

George Bush's postpresidency would have started very early had
it not been for events in the East African nation of Somalia. Its central government had collapsed in 1991, and feuding warlords were
preventing the shipment of desperately needed supplies to the
country's drought-ridden interior. The Bush administration had organized an airlift in early 1992 after the fighting made delivery by
truck impossible. But then the airfields started coming under fire,
and the U.S. forces withdrew. The UN sent five hundred Pakistanis
into the capital, Mogadishu, to move the supplies, and by the late
fall of 1992 they were huddling together under constant fire from
armed gangs.

On November 24 UN secretary-general Boutros Boutros-Ghali
presented a dire picture of the situation to Bush and asked for U.S.
military assistance in opening the truck routes. The criticism of
U.S. inaction in Yugoslavia had stung Bush, who wanted to use U.S.
power in the post–Cold War world for humanitarian reasons, if possible. Yugoslavia was too big and too politically confused for any operation to be simple; but in Somalia the conditions seemed right for
doing this quickly and with few, if any, American casualties. Bush
was also sensitive to the UN secretary-general's argument that
many in the third world were convinced that the reinvigorated Security Council would focus only on the needs of Europeans and

North Americans. Bush found more unity among his advisers for using force in Somalia than anyplace else where the option of using force had been debated in four years. For the first time in any of these discussions, General Colin Powell took the lead in advocating U.S. military intervention. He thought that a small force would make a huge amount of difference and then could pass the mission of keeping the supply lines open to a lightly armed UN group. Many lives would be saved and the entire operation could be completed before January 20, and the U.S. force would be out by March. The goal was to secure the supply lines, not to knit together a Somali state. Bush was easily persuaded—he wanted to make one last contribution for a stronger UN and a better world—and his advisers informed the Clinton transition team that any fighting by U.S. troops in Somalia would be over by Inauguration Day.

As it turned out, the U.S. deployment in Somalia would become an unexpected headache for the Clinton administration, leading to the deaths of eighteen U.S. servicemen in an October 1993 incident later memorialized in the film *Black Hawk Down*. But in another area, Bush's late-term activism would provide positive opportunities to the incoming foreign-policy team. Just after the election, Bush asked Secretary of Commerce Barbara Hackman Franklin, the highest-ranking woman in his administration, to take a trade mission to China. Ministerial contacts between the two countries had been frozen since the Tiananmen Square outrage and Bush wanted to reestablish both governmental exchanges and commercial contacts before he left office. He also wanted to smooth over Beijing's annoyance at the recent sale of U.S. F-16s to Taiwan, which had been authorized during the presidential campaign to make political points in Texas, where the jet fighter aircraft were made. With her visit, Franklin effectively ended the ban on bilateral ministerial discussions and brought home more than a billion dollars in Chinese orders for American manufacturing.

There was another use of presidential power that Bush intended to make. He saw Iran-Contra as a policy failure, not as a crime, and believed that several of Ronald Reagan's advisers had been unfairly prosecuted for doing what they thought was in the national interest. On December 24, 1992, he pardoned former defense secretary Caspar Weinberger and former national security adviser Robert MacFarlane; Elliott Abrams, former assistant secretary of state for inter-American affairs; and former CIA officers Duane Clarridge, Alan Fiers, and Clair George. Some of Bush's closest advisers thought the pardons a mistake because they linked a very successful administration with the errors of its predecessor and raised the old questions about things George Bush might wish to hide. But the outgoing president was adamant that this was the right thing to do. The "common denominator of their motivation—whether their actions were right or wrong—was patriotism," he said in a statement accompanying the pardons. The "criminalization of policy differences," he added, was "a profoundly troubling development in the political and legal climate of our country."

But the pardons also had a direct benefit for Bush. The White House had told Lawrence Walsh of the existence of the Bush diary on December 11, and had Weinberger gone to trial as scheduled on January 6, 1993, the diary, its contents, and Bush's dissembling about Iran-Contra would have been a source of public embarrassment. Bush, in any case, believed that Ronald Reagan should have pardoned these men; since he didn't, Bush would. One last time he felt he had to clean up a mess left by his predecessor.

• • •

After Bill Clinton's inauguration as the forty-second president of the United States, George and Barbara Bush flew to Houston. They planned to build a home in the city, but this retirement had come four years too soon. As evidence of the tenuousness of Bush's Texas roots, his critics had long pointed to the fact that the official residence of this Texan was a rented hotel room in the city. Now it was a rented house.

In the modern era there were two models for a postpresidency. Dwight Eisenhower, Richard Nixon, and Jimmy Carter had stayed active and in the public eye. Herbert Hoover, Harry Truman, Lyndon Johnson, Gerald Ford, and Ronald Reagan had not. Although Bush, whose thyroid disease was now under control, could expect a long postpresidency, he made clear that he expected to retire from public life. "Bill, I want to tell you something. When I leave here, you're going to have no trouble from me," Bush told Clinton in late November 1992. "The campaign is over, it was tough and I'm out of here. I will do nothing to complicate your work and I just want you to know that." Bush was tired of politics, and though he knew that equanimity in defeat was good manners, he was finding it hard not to be bitter about the truncation of his presidency.

The rest of the former first family was less self-conscious about nursing any bitterness for how things had turned out. Barbara Bush vowed not to return to Washington, D.C., anytime soon. When Bill Clinton invited the Bushes in September 1993 to stay the night again in the White House to attend the signing of the peace accord between Israel and the PLO, George Bush said yes but Barbara declined. "It was right and proper that he be there," she confided to her diary. "I am just not ready to go back yet." So the forty-first president returned to Washington and stayed in the White House alone. George Bush also planned to lobby Congress on behalf of the North American Free Trade Agreement (NAFTA), another Clinton achievement whose roots lay in his administration. Bush had signed the agreement with the leaders of Canada and Mexico before leaving office, but the Senate had yet to ratify the treaty. "He is more generous than I am," wrote Barbara. "During the campaign Clinton did not take a side on NAFTA, but now that he needs help he calls on George, Jerry Ford, and Jimmy Carter." The elder sons, George W. and Jeb, shared their mother's anger. In December they had opposed their father's gesture of bringing Dana Carvey to the White House just because they suspected the comedian had voted for Clinton.

. . .

In his first months as an ex-president, George Bush appeared unfocused to his family and closest aides. But he did accept an offer to return with Barbara to the Middle East. In April 1993, they were given a royal tour of Kuwait. In part a money-raising venture—the Kuwaitis would give a lot of money to the new Bush presidential library—this was also an opportunity to bask a little in a great success. "We drove to Bayan Palace and all along the way were people cheering and waving George Bush posters and American flags and Kuwaiti flags," Barbara recounted in her diary. As evidence of the importance of this visit for the former president, he brought a large family contingent. Besides Barbara, he brought sons Marvin and Jeb, and George W.'s wife, Laura. Accompanying the family were former secretary of state James Baker and former Treasury secretary Nicholas Brady.

The Kuwaitis intended to give George Bush their highest award and wanted nothing to interfere with his visit. They therefore hid from their guests and the U.S. secret service, which might well have canceled this trip, the information that days before the American delegation's arrival on April 14 the local authorities had foiled an Iraqi plot to kill the former president. The Kuwaitis arrested seventeen people, some of whom confessed to being on a mission from Baghdad. The plan was to detonate a car bomb, and, indeed, the Kuwaitis found a Toyota Land Cruiser with eighty to ninety kilograms of plastic explosives. Once the Bushes had left, the Kuwaitis informed U.S. authorities, who sent experts to the kingdom to examine the device and interview the captives. Bomb makers leave very distinctive signatures. When the CIA compared the detonator and the remote control trigger to known Iraqi explosives found elsewhere, there was a match. After the FBI gathered some additional corroborating information from the suspects, the Clinton administration concluded without a doubt that Saddam Hussein had authorized the assassination of George Bush. To send a message to Baghdad, Bill Clinton ordered a cruise missile strike on the headquarters of the Iraqi Intelligence Service on June 26, 1993. The next day the U.S. ambassador to the UN, Madeleine Albright, presented evidence of the Iraqi plot to the Security Council. George Bush was the first U.S. president, sitting or former, to be the target of a foreign assassination plot. The significance of that fact would not be fully understood for another decade.

. . .

In early 1994 Barbara Bush's former press secretary Sheila Tate suggested to George Bush that he adopt a cause or project as a former president. "I need more time, more quiet time, more grandchild time, more time to forget and *to remember*," he replied. "I don't have myself cast as a big and important person. I want to be a tiny point of light, hopefully a bright point of light, but I don't crave sitting at the head table; nor do I burn with desire to see that history is kind to us." He expected to need another year and a half of tending to his personal finances—giving speeches primarily. Once Barbara Bush had a nest egg to live off should he predecease her, Bush might indulge in presidential nostalgia. Bush did not change his mind even when two events later made him and Gerald Ford the elder statesmen of the Republican Party. In April Richard Nixon died at age eighty-one, and later that year Ronald Reagan's public voice was stilled by Alzheimer's disease.

It was service to his ambitious sons that was largely responsible for bringing the elder Bush back into the limelight. Still uncomfortable with the press and reluctant to be the focus of attention, the former president nevertheless wanted to help his two eldest sons' fledgling political careers. George W. was campaigning to be governor of Texas, and Jeb had his eyes set on the statehouse in

Florida. Bush agreed to do some campaigning for them, and he also decided to appear on television in the fall with his favorite impersonator, Dana Carvey.

In the spring of 1994 a disagreement over U.S. policy in Haiti had brought Bush's first strong criticism of Bill Clinton's foreign policy. The UN supported using U.S. troops to restore the democratically elected president Jean-Bertrand Aristide to power in Haiti, and the Clinton administration was keeping that option open in the face of heavy congressional pressure to intervene. Calling the use of U.S. ground forces in the impoverished Caribbean country a "tremendous mistake," Bush admitted that he had changed his mind about Aristide. "As president I felt that the way to support democracy in Haiti was to insist on the return of Aristide to power. Given recent events and Aristide's demonstrated instability, the time has come to break the linkage." He wanted the United States to support democracy in Haiti, but not to support Aristide. By the summer of 1994 Bush began peppering his speeches with a much broader criticism of the Clinton administration's foreign policy. He wondered whether this administration understood that the United States did not have an interest in intervening everywhere. "And whether we are talking about Haiti or [North] Korea or the former Soviet Union, the current administration's biggest problem is this: There doesn't seem to be a coherent plan . . . We risk squandering America's leadership all around the world." Bush said he was uncomfortable that America's regional allies Mexico and Argentina opposed the proposed intervention in Haiti. "We must not land troops down there because what that will do is reawaken the agony of the last 40 or 50 years about gunboat diplomacy." Given that only five years earlier he had led an invasion of Panama over the objections of the OAS, Bush's criticism began to seem strained and politically motivated. So, too, did his attacks that summer on Clinton's efforts to reform health care. Until his sons started running for office, Bush had said nothing publicly about Clinton's domestic agenda.

The midterm election of November 4, 1994, brought mixed results for the Bush family. George W. won in Texas, but Jeb lost in Florida. The result was a surprise to the family. While the former president had kept his own counsel, Barbara Bush had tried to persuade George W. not to run against the seemingly popular Democratic governor Ann Richards and assumed until Election Day that her eldest son would lose. Meanwhile Barbara, at least, assumed the more seasoned public speaker and cooler-headed Jeb would be able to best Florida's Lawton Chiles. The results at the national level, however, were less mixed. Although excellent for the Republican Party, in a certain light the outcome of the midterm campaigns spelled a personal repudiation of George Bush. The House was now under the control of the young Republican Turks who had rejected his budget deal. Led by Newt Gingrich, they won promising a Contract with America, which explicitly promised to cut taxes. Implicit in the idea of a contract was the memory of Bush's betrayal of his "read my lips" pledge. A contract was harder to break than a pledge in a political speech.

What public statements Bush made after 1994 were largely nonpartisan and, more often than not, supportive of his successor. Indeed when he spoke out against the rising tide of isolationism, his targets were as much members of his own party as Democrats. "There's a selfishness that says we've done our part, we've kept the peace, let others do their part," Bush said while on a trip to Beijing in September 1995. "How tragic if a selfish world view prevailed . . . We must stay engaged; we must lead." When he issued a statement against intolerance a year later, there was no mistaking that conservatives were his primary focus. In April 1996 white supremacists blew up the Alfred P. Murrah federal building in Oklahoma City, killing 168. Among them was a former secret service agent, Al Whicher, who had worked on Bush's protective detail when he was president and vice president. When the National Rifle Association refused to repudiate attacks on federal law enforcement following the Oklahoma City bombing, Bush decided to resign his life membership of that organization. Al Whicher "was no Nazi," he said. "He was a kind man, a loving parent, a man dedicated to serving his country—and serve it well he did." For Bush there was more than the memory of agent Whicher at issue here. "Your broadside against Federal agents deeply offends my own sense of decency and honor," he wrote to NRA executive vice president Wayne LaPierre in May 1996.

Bush continued to support Clinton's foreign policies whenever he agreed with them, as he had done in strongly advocating a North American free trade pact in 1993. This was not hard for Bush to do, as his successor was also an internationalist and a free trader. On a trip to Hanoi in 1995—leading the highest-level delegation since the end of the Vietnam War—Bush made statements supportive of the Clinton administration's policy of establishing diplomatic relations with Vietnam so long as the Vietnamese committed themselves to building a freer society. "I agree with Secretary of State Warren Christopher," said Bush, "when he talked of a Vietnam more respectful of human rights . . . It must not be our role to try to dictate to Vietnam. But we do have an obligation to state very clearly what we believe, what we feel will help." Bush also gave speeches in support of Clinton's efforts to widen trade with China.

Bush said less about Clinton's domestic policies, but he could not be less than pleased with the complete turnaround in the health of the U.S. budget. Building on the 1990 accord, the Clinton administration reached a compromise budget agreement with Congress in 1993, which created 36 percent and 39.6 percent tax brackets for the wealthiest Americans, raised gasoline taxes, and allowed for more taxation of Social Security benefits. The budget deficit, which had crested at $290 billion in 1992, in the wake of the final bills from the S&L cleanup, went into surplus in 1998 for the first time in nearly thirty years.

Throughout his presidency, George Bush had made comments

about how he might be viewed by historians. But as a former president he showed little interest in moving the process along and fellow Republicans had almost no interest in defining a Bush legacy. "He was an ineffective one-term president," said longtime Reagan aide Lyn Nofziger in 1995. "[H]e walked away from the Reagan legacy and tried to create his own—and failed at that." Bush found himself once again in Reagan's shadow. In 1997 a nationwide Ronald Reagan Legacy Project established the goal of naming something—a bridge, a highway, a park—for Reagan in every one of the United States' 3,067 counties. There was nothing similar for Bush, although after Washington's National Airport was renamed the Ronald Reagan airport, Houston's international airport was named after Bush. Later the CIA's headquarters in Langley, Virginia, came to bear his name. Although he had spent only a year there, Bush's CIA experience marked him for life and left him with a deep emotional attachment to that institution.

The most important Bush building was, of course, his presidential library and the George Bush School established next to it in 1997. In 1994 he had decided that the complex would be built at Texas A&M University in College Station. Although far from Houston and not previously affiliated with the Bush family, the university had made a very strong bid for Bush's 40 million pages of presidential records and personal memorabilia, and both of the Bushes felt very comfortable there. Indeed, after witnessing the funeral of Richard Nixon at the site of his then private library in Yorba Linda, the former president and first lady decided they wanted to be buried in College Station.

Besides his involvement with the library, Bush made only minor efforts to shape his legacy. In October 1995 he held a gathering of what he liked to call the "used to bes," François Mitterrand, Margaret Thatcher, Mikhail Gorbachev, and Canada's Brian Mulroney, to discuss the end of the Cold War. Although still careful not to criticize Reagan, Bush distanced himself from conservatives who argued that Reagan policies, particularly the Strategic Defense Initiative, had influenced Gorbachev's critical decisions. In response to Margaret Thatcher's claim that SDI was "a vital factor" in bringing about the end of the Cold War, Bush said, "I would differ with Margaret on the degree of importance in terms of, you might say, compelling the rapid change inside the Soviet Union." Gorbachev agreed, saying, "If you accept that reforms in the Soviet Union started under the pressure from the West, particularly under the pressure of the implementation of SDI, I think that would distort the real picture." When asked about the reunification of Germany, Gorbachev explained that it "was one of the most difficult questions after our domestic processes," and he credited the two-plus-four talks and the panoply of security and border treaties negotiated in the diplomatic process led by the Bush administration for making a reunited Germany in NATO easier to accept: "that created greater confidence for the Soviet Union and other countries that the process will be within this framework of overall improvement of our cooperation and improvement in trust."

Oddly, the action that had the greatest influence on Bush's public appeal in the second half of the 1990s involved jumping out of an airplane at 12,500 feet. Early in 1997 Bush was guest of honor at the annual meeting of the International Parachute Association. There he told the sad story of the day he bailed out of his fiery Navy Avenger in 1944 and left two of his crewmates behind in the doomed bomber. "As I recounted these errors," Bush wrote the next day to his children, "something happened. For some reason, I went back to a thought I had way in the back of my mind. It has been there, sleeping like Rip van Winkle, alive but not alive. Now it was quite clear. I want to make one more parachute jump!" Bush hadn't yet told Barbara and expected resistance but, as he explained to his kids, "in the final analysis I will convince her (1) that it is safe and (2) that this is something I have to do, must do." Bush faced even greater resistance from Colin Powell, who was used to trying to discourage the old man from deploying U.S. military assets. Bush hoped to jump with the U.S. Army's Golden Knights. "Are you planning to jump from a plane?" asked Powell. "It's the talk of the Pentagon." He then continued, "I know you look 45, but you're 72. How are your ankles, knees, etc?" Bush went ahead with the preparation. Eleven days before the jump, or J Day, he called each of his children. "Are you kidding, Dad?" was the first response of Marvin and George W., followed by enthusiasm. Jeb Bush, who hated to chatter about anything, responded with a one-liner: "Fine, Dad, but don't change your sexual preference." "I put him down as positive," noted his father.

Bush dropped about half a century in age on J Day, March 25, 1997. He learned the jumpers' secret handshake, which ended with index fingers pointed at each other, signaling pull the rip cord. "I got caught up in the spirit of it all—totally hyped," he said. Bush wore his Desert Storm boots and what he referred to as his "white Elvis suit (with white helmet and white gloves—the King would have approved)." The jump was a success. "The floating to earth took longer than I thought, but I wish it could have gone on twice as long . . . I didn't hit hard, but a gust of wind seemed to pull me back . . . I was down. It had gone well. I had lived a dream." Then Barbara hugged him. "All was well with the world." Covered by newspapers and on television around the world, the jump revealed a different George Bush than the stiff and awkward man who had served as president for four years.

That is not to say that his former lieutenants were as uninterested in history's verdict as he was. In early 1993 they had formed a "Book Group," which included Scowcroft and Condoleezza Rice, the newly minted provost of Stanford University who had been a senior director in the Bush National Security Council, to have him focus on writing some sort of memoir. His former aides also encouraged him to support an oral history project sponsored by the Miller Center of Public Affairs at the University of Virginia, though he was reluctant to be interviewed for it. Instead of a memoir, he decided to collaborate with Scowcroft and a young staffer-historian named James McCall on a book about his administration's handling of the Soviet Union and the Gulf War. The book was a literary platypus, containing first-person sections by Bush and Scowcroft, including many direct excerpts from the former president's contemporaneous diary entries. The Bush diaries proved a rich vein of information and offered a window into an emotional and introspective Bush that few had known as president. In 1999, a year after the publication of the Bush-Scowcroft book (*A World Transformed*), a collection of other diary entries and Bush's letters from World War II to 1998 was published as *All the Best, George Bush*. Throughout his presidency, Bush had resisted efforts by speechwriters and senior staffers to substitute flowery language for his own somewhat fractured syntax. In rejecting the modern convention that presidents produce memoirs written by staff or literary hired guns, Bush preferred to speak for himself in letters and diary entries instead of having someone create an artificial narrative.

As the next generation of Bushes vied for greater national prominence, George Bush's legacy was more a burden than an advantage, especially in the Republican Party. The canonization of Ronald Reagan was accompanied by a general contempt for George Bush among conservatives. "The far right will continue to accuse me of 'Betraying the Reagan Revolution'—something Ronald Reagan would never do," Bush confessed with dismay to his elder sons. At the dedication ceremony of the Bush library in November 1997, Governor George W. Bush had made a case for what history might do for his father. "Here, objective historians will look at his record and conclude President Bush was a man who knew his priorities and never wavered from them. President Bush was a man who entered the political arena and left with his integrity intact. President Bush was a leader who stared tyranny in the face and never blinked. George Bush was a great President of the United States of America because he is first and foremost a great man." But that day seemed very far away.

In 1998, with both Jeb and George W. running again, George

Bush understood that his sons worried about the attacks that their father's legacy was taking in their campaigns. "So read my lips—no more worrying," wrote their father in August 1998. He set them free, perhaps as even his own father had not done for him. "At some point both of you may want to say, 'Well, I don't agree with Dad on that point,' or 'Frankly I think Dad was wrong on that.' Do it. Chart your own course, not just on the issues but on defining your-selves. No one will ever question your love of family—your devo-tion to your parents. We have all lived long enough and lived in a way that demonstrates our closeness; so do not worry when the comparisons might be hurtful to your Dad for nothing can ever be written that will drive a wedge between us—nothing at all." George H. W. Bush had turned his back on Prescott Bush's moder-ate Republican views in his effort to win in Texas in 1964, and he expected the same competitive spirit from his own sons.

The elections of 1998 brought a second Bush son into a state-house. As Barbara Bush liked to crow, Jeb Bush's election as gover-nor of Florida meant that one in eight Americans lived in a state governed by a member of the family. George W.'s landslide victory in Texas had even greater implications. As the first Texan reelected to consecutive terms as governor in a quarter of a century, Bush immediately became a front-runner for the Republican presiden-tial nomination in 2000, along with Arizona senator John McCain and former vice president Dan Quayle. His parents were immedi-ately supportive.

At the end of the 1992 campaign the elder George Bush had noted that it was "a joy having George with us—feisty fighter and campaigner if there ever was one." The relationship between father and son had not always been easy, and its inner workings were largely hidden from outsiders. George W. shared his father's intense competitiveness and emotionalism, but he didn't try to restrain these traits. And if young Bush had the voice of grandmother Dorothy Walker Bush in his ear, he wasn't listening. This difference in personal conduct was most noticeable on the matter of religion. Both men were deeply committed Christians. Bush's Episcopalian faith was cool though ever present and grounding. By contrast, following a hard-drinking, hard-partying adolescence that stretched until age forty, George W. had embraced evangelical Christianity and pledged himself born-again to family friend Billy Graham. Whereas the father's efforts to attract Christian conservatives had been awkward for all concerned, the younger Bush easily spoke from the heart about Jesus Christ. More than anything else, this cultural difference overcame the traditional skepticism of the Bush family on the part of conservatives. After George W. won the 2000 South Carolina primary and then the nomination, it appeared that the son had healed the breach in the Republican Party between fiscal and cultural conservatives that was created under the father.

George and Barbara Bush campaigned hard for their son in 2000. Barbara participated in countless coffee hours with women throughout the country, while George tapped his widespread network to raise money. In New Hampshire the Gregg family helped the son as they had the father (though George W. would lose the primary), and the pattern of the son building upon the father's network held elsewhere. As the campaign progressed, Barbara Bush was once again the family pessimist while the former president and his eldest sons thought that the family would win. Barbara couldn't bear to listen to press criticism of her son, whereas George followed everything he could. This created some tension between the former first couple, and George agreed to use wireless earphones around the house so that he could continue to follow television accounts while his wife could ignore the muted sets. The father also watched all of the debates, and though they brought back bad memories he cheered on his son. Barbara couldn't bring herself to watch.

On election night they were with the candidate and extended family in Austin, Texas. When some of the networks declared the key swing state of Florida for Vice President Al Gore, the group was crestfallen. Jeb, who had worked hard to deliver his home state to his brother, was shocked and depressed. "Jeb came over to his brother and said that he had let him down and they hugged," recalled his mother. George W., who had been supremely confident of victory, excused himself and told Laura that he wanted to watch the rest of the results come in at the Governor's Mansion. The inner family, including the elder Bushes, followed and stayed up into the early morning, watching Florida seesaw and their son be declared president-elect for a brief moment. Throughout the night George Bush's face was the family's picture of Dorian Gray, growing older and more haggard as the news became less hopeful. When dawn broke, the country lacked a president-elect and the Bushes were in limbo between victory and defeat. Al Gore had won 500,000 votes more than Bush, but neither candidate had garnered the 270 electoral votes needed to be declared president. The irony was rich and improbable. George W.'s political fate rested on a recount in Governor Jeb Bush's state of Florida. Jeb recused himself from the recount, and honorary presidential uncle James Baker led a team of lawyers in behalf of George W. Bush in Florida. The recount took thirty-six days, with the ultimate decision made by the U.S. Supreme Court in *Bush v. Gore*. George Bush's Supreme Court justices split on whether to allow the recount to continue in Florida: David Souter for and Clarence Thomas against. There were historical ironies everywhere. The last time the son of a president had himself become president, his victory followed an indeterminate election (in which he had lost the popular vote) that had to be determined by the U.S. House of Representatives. John Quincy Adams never escaped the taint of what became known as the "corrupt bargain." George W. hoped for better.

· · ·

On January 20, 2001, the new president, Bush 43, wanted his first visitor in the Oval Office to be his father, Bush 41. The elder man was having a hot bath in the family quarters of the White House when he was told that "the president" wished to see him. He leaped up, dressed, and in one of his proudest moments George Bush left for the Oval Office. What followed was very emotional for both men. The new president later described the scene to his mother: "He knew how much this would mean to his dad, and he wanted to share his first moments in this revered office with him." As a sign of respect for his son and a symbol of the end of his own political career, the former president made it known that to eliminate public confusion he should be referred to as George H. W. Bush, the full, patrician name that he had stopped using forty years earlier when he entered politics.

There hadn't been a father-son combination since 1825. But John Adams was older than Bush by more than a decade when his son became president and would live only a year into John Quincy Adams's term. The more interesting comparison was to another, more recent father-son combination from Massachusetts. Joseph Kennedy was enormously proud of his son John F. Kennedy. Kennedy and the elder Bush were contemporaries and navy veterans of the Pacific war. Joseph Kennedy and his son had very different political views. The father was fiscally conservative and tended to be isolationist. Although a stroke in 1961 robbed the presidential father of any further opportunities to influence his son, there was always speculation about the father's influence in shaping the president that his son became.

Much was made during the campaign of George W.'s ignorance of foreign affairs. His tutor, Condoleezza Rice, tried to point out to journalists that as governor of a border state, George W. had an understanding of the complex relationship with Mexico, but after the candidate in an interview in 1999 could not name the leaders of India or Pakistan, there seemed little reason to believe that he had inherited his father's love of foreign relations.

The assumption that the younger Bush would reconstitute his

father's foreign policy team took some of the edge off Democratic criticisms of his inexperience. The "adults" would be in charge was a mantra for many in the Washington establishment who saw Bush as little more than a frat boy who had sailed through life on his father's coattails. The assumption, however, that the new Bush administration would revive the successful foreign policy of the previous one was based on a fundamental misunderstanding of how George H. W. Bush's administration had worked. The advisers rarely agreed. When it came to the big decisions—whether to push for a reunified Germany in NATO; whether to commit the United States to liberate Kuwait; whether to fire on an Iraqi tanker before getting UN approval; whether to seek congressional authorization for the war; whether to start Desert Storm—Bush made the decisions himself. Indeed the only big foreign policy decision that emerged through consensus was the decision to stop the Gulf War at midnight on February 28, 1991, the most controversial foreign policy decision of that administration.

In its first moments the George W. Bush administration also acquired a different tone. Condoleezza Rice was the new Brent Scowcroft. She, too, was personally close to the president but unlike Scowcroft was not considered a peer by the other foreign policy principals. Colin Powell was the new James Baker. Powell was nowhere near as close to the new President Bush as Baker had been to his father. Powell was also a natural follower of civilian leaders and would not be capable of holding off his rivals in the cabinet as Baker had done in August 1990 over the issue of what to do about the Iraqi tanker. Dick Cheney was back, but this time in a much stronger position. Under George H. W. Bush, Cheney had won a few minor skirmishes on arms control positions and the defense budget until changes in the Soviet Union made his hawkishness seem quaint. On the big strategic questions, Cheney always lost. But in the new Bush administration, Cheney—now vice president—had an ally that he had lacked before. The new secretary of defense,

Donald Rumsfeld, had been Cheney's boss in the Nixon and Ford administrations. Rumsfeld and the elder Bush disliked each other and had long been political rivals. Rumsfeld barely tried to hide his contempt for George H. W. Bush and did not serve in any capacity in that administration. But with the younger Bush a neophyte in foreign policy and willing to defer to his vice president, Rumsfeld gained enormous influence. The result was that the new administration was not a restoration of the old one. Its priorities in foreign policy reflected those of Cheney and Rumsfeld, not George H. W. Bush, Baker, and Scowcroft.

The consequences of this shift from the ways of the father came early. Between 1993 and 1999 the elder Bushes visited China nine times. The former president went on junkets to help American companies establish themselves in this fast-developing economy. Barbara Bush joined a Hong Kong businessman in developing a neighborhood northwest of the Forbidden City in Beijing. Yet the new administration decried Chinese global ambitions and spoke of Beijing's threatening military. The first George Bush administration played down missile defense, assuming that Ronald Reagan's "star wars" dreams were destabilizing and technologically unattainable. In the mid-1990s Donald Rumsfeld had been the chairman of a private panel that advocated accelerating the deployment of U.S. missile defenses and discarding the Anti-Ballistic Missile Treaty with Russia. Cheney, who had seen the ease with which Iraq hid and fired its missiles in the Gulf War, shared this concern about the consequences of the proliferation of missile technology. The George W. Bush team lost no time in its first months renouncing the ABM treaty despite Russian reluctance. Going along with the foreign policy priorities of his advisers, the new president seemed to be preoccupied with domestic matters. The younger Bush's Lee Atwater was Karl Rove, a political adviser who combined Atwater's sense for the jugular with a broad historical perspective. Rove and Bush decided to establish the new administration's credibility with the conservative voters very quickly. In early 2001 they sent to Congress a request for a huge tax cut, not only rolling back marginal rates to where they had been at the time of the 1990 budget agreement but instituting a huge reduction in estate taxes. In the summer they decided to use a controversy over whether the federal government should sponsor research on cells taken from the brain stems of fetuses to establish Bush as the most "pro-life" president in U.S. history. On August 9, 2001, George W. Bush's first speech to the nation was on stem cell research. Foreign policy was expected to stay in the background.

. . .

George and Barbara Bush woke up in the White House on September 11, 2001. Their son was in Florida, where he was planning to visit a school to demonstrate his commitment to education. First lady Laura Bush, who was hosting her in-laws, also had education policy on her mind that morning. She was expecting to testify to Congress that day on the issue. The elder Bushes left early to fly to St. Paul, Minnesota, to give speeches before returning to Houston. On the private plane, which was diverted to Milwaukee, Wisconsin, the former president learned that terrorists had flown two commercial planes into the World Trade Center in New York City. From the Secret Service, he and Barbara were also told that their son and Laura were safe. Only later did they learn that it was their son Marvin who had been closest to death that horrific morning. As the buildings collapsed, he was stuck in a halted subway car underneath Wall Street.

George Bush reacted to this crisis as he had to those he had faced as president. He began to talk to people, though this time they were somewhat startled average Americans at a mall in Milwaukee where the Secret Service had driven the Bushes to buy some walking shoes. He also talked to people on a public golf course, where the couple later went for a walk, and found himself comforting people at dinner at a family restaurant that night. The next day, an exception to the closure of U.S. airspace was made for the elder Bushes, who were flown to Kennebunkport.

George W. Bush told his mother that what she could do for the country at this moment was go out and "BUY! BUY! BUY!" His father thought little of this idea and suggested going out on the lawn and singing patriotic songs. Meanwhile George W. rallied the nation for a war against al Qaeda, the terrorist group led by Osama bin Laden that had organized the attacks on the twin towers and the Pentagon, and the Taliban regime that had provided sanctuary to al Qaeda in Afghanistan.

A year later, following the collapse of the Taliban regime, the country found itself embroiled in a debate over what to do about Iraq. Vice President Cheney was convinced that Saddam Hussein had somehow been involved in helping al Qaeda. Meanwhile Rumsfeld believed that in the post-9/11 world the United States had a duty to dispatch, wherever possible, any snakes in the grass lest they attack first. George W. Bush shared his father's emotionalism about Saddam. In January 2002 he included Iraq along with North Korea and Iran in an "Axis of Evil." In a September 2002 interview the elder George Bush admitted to long hating Saddam. "I don't hate a lot of people. I don't hate easily," he said. Yet he said he had no second thoughts about his decision to halt the war in 1991. "My only regret is that I was wrong, as was every other leader, in thinking that Saddam Hussein would be gone." In the late 1990s, President Hosni Mubarak had invited Bush, Cheney, and Scowcroft to visit Egypt. During that trip the men had discussed whether they should have handled the Gulf War differently, and all agreed, even Cheney, that they had managed the ending of the war properly.

The media made much of the father's reluctance to second-guess his 1991 decision and what that might mean for his assessment of his son's handling of the tyrant a decade later. In the summer of

2002 Brent Scowcroft published an op-ed article in the *Wall Street Journal* that argued against invading and occupying Iraq for many of the same reasons that he had given in 1991. And it was assumed that he was a stalking horse for the first president Bush. As he had done as Reagan's vice president, the elder Bush hid his thoughts about current U.S. policy from public view. Meanwhile his son was evasive about what, if any, advice he was receiving from his father. In a rambling interview with the celebrated journalist Bob Woodward, George W. Bush used misdirection to obscure the advice he had received from his father. "I'm not trying to be evasive. I don't remember. I could ask him and see if he remembers something . . . The discussions would be more on the tactics. How are we doing, How are you doing with the Brits? He is following the news now. And so I am briefing him on what I see. You know, he is the wrong father to appeal to in terms of strength. There is a higher father that I appeal to." The latter comment drew headlines, but George W. had actually refused to discuss his father's role.

It is a safe assumption that George H. W. Bush supported Colin Powell's effort to delay the start of the war and build an international coalition against Saddam. Unlike in 1990–91, the United States failed a decade later to enlist the support of the Russians, the French, the Germans, the Canadians, or the Egyptians and had to trumpet a group of mainly weaker allies—the "coalition of the willing"—that included Albania, Armenia, Tonga, and Thailand. The military coalition was also less than half the size of what the first Bush administration had assembled. Only four allies—Australia, Denmark, Great Britain, and Poland—supplied troops to the initial invasion force of 300,000. And of that total the United States had provided 250,000.

But it is also a safe assumption that the elder Bush was eager to see the end of Saddam Hussein. The Bush family no doubt cheered when Saddam Hussein was found in a spider hole in December 2003. In 1991, after the embarrassment of trying to find Manuel

Noriega in Panama, Bush and his advisers had predicted that it would take a long time to capture Saddam, if they tried. Despite the U.S. occupation of Iraq, it took his son's administration eight months to arrest the dictator.

. . .

George W.'s victory over Senator John Kerry of Massachusetts in the 2004 presidential election sealed the Bush family's claim to being one of the most successful political dynasties in U.S. history: two presidents (one term and two terms), two governors, one senator, and a congressman. Yet over the course of his long public life, George Bush had witnessed the fragility of second terms. Although he did not get one, himself, Bush had seen close-up the collapse of three presidencies in their second term. Lyndon Johnson's administration foundered on Vietnam, Richard Nixon's on Watergate, and Ronald Reagan's on Iran-Contra.

George W. Bush's second term quickly began to display the characteristics of other failed presidencies. In Iraq the number of American casualties mounted as did sectarian violence and U.S. domestic opposition. Meanwhile, while earning credit for five years without a terrorist attack in the United States, the administration came under fire for counterterrorism measures involving domestic surveillance and the use of torture on suspects and their detention without trial. The supposed influence of Vice President Cheney was blamed for the administration's apparent nostalgia for an earlier era when the White House felt it could wiretap, deploy troops, and conduct covert operations at will.

Nostalgia for George H. W. Bush's presidency rose as his son's popularity declined. Some critics of the Iraq War wondered why the son had not been persuaded by the logic that had kept his father from going into Baghdad a decade earlier. Others wondered whether the U.S. military had lost whatever chance it had to establish order because the son's administration had used half the number of troops for its invasion in 2003 as had the father in 1990–91. Meanwhile the elder Bush's public profile increased after his son's reelection. Following a devastating tsunami in late December 2004 that killed approximately 275,000 in Asia, George W. enlisted his father and former president Bill Clinton to raise money for relief. The years had softened whatever anger remained between George H. W. Bush and the former rival, and following this joint mission the two former presidents became very friendly. Clinton vacationed at Kennebunkport in June 2005 and had started calling Barbara Bush "Mom." When Hurricane Katrina devastated New Orleans and southern Mississippi two months later, the close relationship between Clinton and the elder Bush was again highlighted as once more George W. Bush asked these two men to lead a charitable campaign to help the victims.

Hurricane Katrina was a reminder of how little presidential administrations learn from one another, even when they involve many of the same people. In 1992 the first Bush administration had discovered that local authorities lacked the resources to handle widespread catastrophes. Indeed, Andrew Card, the man who as George H. W. Bush's personal representative in August 1992 had pushed the governor of Florida to accept U.S. troops in the wake of Hurricane Andrew, was now White House chief of staff, and Dick Cheney, who had organized that relief effort as secretary of defense, was now vice president; yet for days in late August and early September 2005, the people of New Orleans lived and died in the muck. Over one thousand would ultimately perish before the U.S. military finally established order, brought in supplies, and provided shelter.

The country's fiscal situation also inspired comparisons between the two presidents Bush. The son had sought to avoid his father's political fate by lowering taxes and keeping them low. As was predictable, this policy led to the same budget difficulties that had caused George H. W. Bush to break his "no new taxes" pledge in the first place. In Bill Clinton's last year in office, the federal government had a $260 billion surplus. Following the first round of the younger Bush's budget cuts, the federal budget went into deficit in 2002 ($158 billion) for the first time in four years. After hitting a record deficit of $413 billion in 2005, the figure settled below the $200 billion mark in Bush's second term, approximately what it had been when in 1990 his father made his toughest political decision.

When George W. Bush had spoken confidently in 1997 of how history would revise his father's reputation, he had no reason to assume that it would be because of his own shortcomings as president. Yet the second father-son presidential act in U.S. history produced something the first pairing did not. George W. Bush's controversial presidency led to a positive reassessment of his father's time in the White House. A decade later, as the younger Bush's own presidency limped to an end, many missed the elder Bush's realism, his diplomacy, his political modesty, and, yes, even his prudence. George H. W. Bush had proved himself up to the challenges, foreign and domestic, of the end of the Cold War, and now many wondered whether his style of leadership was also right for whatever war it was that the United States now found itself in. And, ironically, many also wished that someone like the elder Bush could come on the scene to clean up his son's mess in Washington as he had once done for Ronald Reagan.

Milestones

1924	George Herbert Walker Bush is born on June 12 in Milton, Massachusetts
1942	Enlists in the United States Navy on his eighteenth birthday after graduating from Phillips Academy, Andover
1943	Becomes youngest aviator in the U.S. Navy
1944	Shot down over the island of Chichi Jima
1945	Marries Barbara Pierce on January 6
1946	Son George W. Bush is born
1948	Graduates from Yale College and moves to Odessa, Texas
1949	Daughter Pauline Robinson (Robin) Bush is born
1950	Bush and his family move to Midland, Texas
1953	Son John Ellis (Jeb) Bush is born
	Becomes cofounder, with Hugh and Bill Liedtke, of Zapata Petroleum
	Three-year-old daughter Robin dies of cancer
1955	Son Neil Mallon Bush is born
1956	Son Marvin Pierce Bush is born
1959	Moves to Houston, Texas, to run Zapata Offshore
	Daughter Dorothy Ellis (Doro) Bush is born
1963	Elected chairman of the Harris County Republican Party
1964	Loses Texas Senate race to Ralph Yarborough
1966	Elected to Congress from Texas's Seventh District
1968	Reelected to Congress
1970	Loses Texas Senate race to Lloyd Bentsen
1971	Becomes U.S. permanent representative to the United Nations
1973	Becomes chairman of the Republican National Committee
1974	President Richard Nixon resigns from office and is replaced by Gerald R. Ford

	Becomes chief of the U.S. Liaison Office in Beijing
1976	Becomes director of Central Intelligence
1977	Inauguration of Jimmy Carter as president; leaves CIA and returns to Texas
1979	Announces candidacy for president of the United States in Washington
1980	Selected as Ronald Reagan's running mate; elected vice president
1981	Attempted assassination of Ronald Reagan
1984	Reagan and Bush are reelected
1986	Iran-Contra scandal breaks
1987	Announces candidacy for president of the United States in Houston
1988	Selects Senator J. Danforth "Dan" Quayle of Indiana as his running mate; elected president in race against Governor Michael Dukakis of Massachusetts
1989	Inaugurated as the forty-first president of the United States on January 20
	Chinese army uses force against demonstrators in Beijing's Tiananmen Square on June 4
	Visits Poland and Hungary
	Signs the Financial Institutions Reform, Recovery, and Enforcement Act of 1989 to resolve the S&L crisis
	Berlin Wall falls on November 9
	Summit with Soviet leader Mikhail Gorbachev in Malta
	U.S. forces invade Panama on December 20
1990	Panamanian leader Manuel Noriega surrenders to U.S. authorities in Panama City on January 3
	The Supreme Council of Lithuania proclaims Lithuanian independence
	Summit with Mikhail Gorbachev in Washington, D.C.
	Publicly revokes his "Read My Lips" pledge in a written statement released to the press on June 26
	Nominates David Souter to the Supreme Court
	Signs the Americans with Disabilities Act
	Iraq invades Kuwait on August 2; the UN Security Council passes Resolution 660 demanding Iraq's immediate withdrawal; U.S. and USSR issue joint statement on Iraqi aggression in the Gulf
	Bush announces on August 5, "This will not stand, this aggression against Kuwait"
	Operation Desert Shield deploys U.S. and coalition troops to Saudi Arabia

Bush and congressional leaders announce a bipartisan budget agreement on September 30

West and East Germany are united on October 3

Signs the Budget Enforcement Act of 1990

Signs the Clean Air Act of 1990

United States signs the Conventional Forces in Europe (CFE) Treaty along with the Soviet Union and twenty former members of NATO and the Warsaw Pact

1991   U.S. Congress authorizes use of force to liberate Kuwait on January 12; air war of Operation Desert Storm begins on January 17; ground war begins on February 24

Bush suspends combat operations at midnight (EST) on February 28 after the liberation of Kuwait

Nominates Clarence Thomas to the Supreme Court

Signs START with Gorbachev in Moscow

Coup attempt against Gorbachev in Moscow on August 19–22

Signs the Civil Rights Act of 1991

Gorbachev resigns on December 25; the Soviet Union dissolves

1992   Attends the Earth Summit in Rio de Janeiro and supports the climate change convention

Hurricane Andrew hits south Florida on August 24

Loses presidential election to Democratic nominee William Jefferson Clinton in a three-way race involving Ross Perot

Announces Operation Restore Hope in Somalia

1993   Signs START II with Russian president Boris Yeltsin

Presidential term ends; returns to private life in Houston

1994   George W. Bush is elected governor of Texas; Jeb Bush is defeated in the governor's race in Florida

1998   George W. Bush is reelected governor of Texas and Jeb Bush is elected governor of Florida

2000   George W. Bush is elected the forty-third president of the United States

2001   Al Qaeda launches attacks on the United States

2003   The United States invades Iraq

2004   George W. Bush is reelected president

An earthquake in the Indian Ocean on December 26 creates a tsunami that kills more than 275,000 people in Asia; President George W. Bush asks his father and former president Clinton to head a major effort to raise voluntary contributions

2005   Hurricane Katrina hits New Orleans and the coast of Mississippi on August 29; again former presidents Bush and Clinton cooperate to help the needy

Selected Bibliography

MEMOIRS AND DIARIES

Baker, James (with Thomas M. DeFrank). *The Politics of Diplomacy: Revolution, War and Peace, 1989–1992.* New York: G. P. Putnam's Sons, 1995.

Bush, Barbara. *A Memoir.* New York: Scribner, 1994.

———. *Reflections: Life After the White House.* New York: Scribner, 2003.

Bush, George. *All the Best, George Bush: My Life in Letters and Other Writings.* New York: Scribner, 1999.

——— (with Vic Gold). *Looking Forward: An Autobiography.* New York: Bantam, 1988.

———, and Brent Scowcroft. *A World Transformed.* New York: Knopf, 1998.

Chernayev, Anatoly C. *My Six Years with Gorbachev.* University Park, Pa.: Penn State University Press, 2000.

Connally, John (with Mickey Herskowitz). *In History's Shadow: An American Odyssey.* New York: Hyperion, 1993.

Darman, Richard. *Who's in Control?: Polar Politics and the Sensible Center.* New York: Simon and Schuster, 1996.

Ford, Gerald. *A Time to Heal: The Autobiography of Gerald R. Ford.* New York: Harper and Row, 1979.

Gates, Robert M. *From the Shadows: The Ultimate Insider's Story of Five Presidents and How They Won the Cold War.* New York: Simon and Schuster, 1996.

Haldeman, H. R. *The Haldeman Diaries: Inside the Nixon White House.* New York: G. P. Putnam's Sons, 1994.

Kissinger, Henry A. *White House Years.* Boston: Little, Brown, 1979.

Novak, Robert D. *The Prince of Darkness: 50 Years of Reporting in Washington.* New York: Crown Forum, 2007.

Quayle, Dan. *Standing Firm: A Vice-Presidential Memoir.* New York: HarperCollins/Zondervan, 1994.

Reagan, Nancy. *My Turn: The Memoirs of Nancy Reagan* (with William Novak). New York: Random House, 1989.

Reagan, Ronald. *An American Life.* New York: Simon and Schuster, 1990.

———. *The Reagan Diaries.* Edited by Douglas Brinkley. New York: HarperCollins, 2007.

Regan, Donald T. *For the Record: From Wall Street to Washington.* New York: Harcourt Brace Jovanovich, 1988.

Rubin, Robert E., and Jacob Weisberg. *In an Uncertain World: Tough Choices from Wall Street to Washington.* New York: Random House, 2003.

Scheer, Robert. *Playing President: My Close Encounters with Nixon, Carter, Bush I, Reagan, and Clinton—and How They Did Not Prepare Me for George W. Bush.* New York: Akashic Books, 2006.

Shultz, George. *Turmoil and Triumph: My Years as Secretary of State.* New York: Charles Scribner's Sons, 1993.

Thompson, Kenneth, ed. *The Bush Presidency: Ten Intimate Perspectives of George Bush.* Portraits of American Presidents, vol. 10. Lanham, Md.: University Press of America, 1997.

SECONDARY SOURCES

Allen, Steven J., and Richard A. Viguerie. *Lip Service: George Bush's 30-Year Battle with Conservatives.* Chantilly, Va.: CP Books, 1992.

Beschloss, Michael, and Strobe Talbott. *At the Highest Levels: The Inside Story of the End of the Cold War.* Boston: Little, Brown, 1993.

Brinkley, Douglas. *The Unfinished Presidency: Jimmy Carter's Journey Beyond the White House.* New York: Viking, 1998.

Busch, Andrew E. *Reagan's Victory: The Presidential Election of 1980 and the Rise of the Right.* Lawrence.: University Press of Kansas, 2005.

Cannon, Lou. *Governor Reagan: His Rise to Power.* New York: PublicAffairs, 2003.

———. *President Reagan: The Role of a Lifetime.* New York: PublicAffairs, 2000.

DeYoung, Karen. *Soldier: The Life of Colin Powell.* New York: Knopf, 2006.

Duffy, Michael, and Dan Goodgame. *Marching in Place: The Status Quo Presidency of George Bush.* New York: Simon and Schuster, 1992.

Fursenko, Aleksandr, and Timothy Naftali. *Khrushchev's Cold War: The Inside Story of an American Adversary.* New York: Norton, 2006.

Kabaservice, Geoffrey. *The Guardians: Kingman Brewster, His Circle, and the Rise of the Liberal Establishment.* New York: Henry Holt, 2004.

Kelley, Kitty. *The Family: The Real Story of the Bush Dynasty.* New York: Anchor Books, 2005.

Koch, Doro Bush. *My Father, My President: A Personal Account of the Life of George H. W. Bush.* New York: Warner Books, 2006.

LeoGrande, William M. *Our Own Backyard: The United States in Central America, 1977–1992.* Chapel Hill: University of North Carolina Press, 1998.

Litan, Robert E., and Jonathan Rauch. *American Finance for the 21st Century.* Washington, D.C.: Brookings Institution, 1998.

Lukas, J. Anthony. *Nightmare: The Underside of the Nixon Years.* Athens: Ohio University Press, 1999.

Naftali, Timothy. *Blind Spot: The Secret History of American Counterterrorism.* New York: Basic Books, 2005.

Noonan, Peggy. *When Character Was King: A Story of Ronald Reagan.* New York: Penguin, 2001.

Oberdorfer, Don. *From the Cold War to a New Era: The United States and the Soviet Union, 1983–1991.* Updated edition. Baltimore: Johns Hopkins University Press, 1998.

Parmet, Herbert S. *George Bush: The Life of a Lone Star Yankee.* New York: Scribner, 1997.

Patterson, James T. *Grand Expectations: The United States, 1945–1974.* New York: Oxford University Press, 1996.

———. *Restless Giant: The United States from Watergate to Bush v. Gore.* New York: Oxford University Press, 2005.

Perlstein, Rick. *Before the Storm: Barry Goldwater and the Unmaking of the American Consensus.* New York: Hill and Wang, 2001.

Phillips, Kevin. *Boiling Point: Democrats, Republicans and the Decline of Middle-Class Prosperity.* New York: HarperPerennial, 1994.

———. *The Politics of Rich and Poor: Wealth and the American Electorate in the Reagan Aftermath.* New York: Random House, 1990.

Pollack, Kenneth. *The Persian Puzzle: The Conflict Between Iran and America.* New York: Random House, 2004.

———. *The Threatening Storm: The Case for Invading Iraq.* New York: Random House, 2002.

Prados, John. *Keepers of the Keys: A History of the National Security Council from Truman to Bush.* New York: William Morrow, 1991.

———. *Safe for Democracy: The Secret Wars of the CIA.* Chicago: Ivan R. Dee, 2006.

Ranelagh, John. *The Agency: The Rise and Decline of the CIA.* Revised edition. New York: Simon and Schuster, 1987.

Rapoport, Ronald B., and Walter J. Stone. *Three's a Crowd: The Dynamic of Third Parties, Ross Perot, and Republican Resurgence.* Ann Arbor: University of Michigan Press, 2005.

Schweizer, Peter, and Rochelle Schweizer. *The Bushes: Portrait of a Dynasty.* New York: Doubleday, 2004.

Wicker, Tom. *George Herbert Walker Bush: A Penguin Life.* New York: Viking, 2004.

Woodward, Bob. *The Agenda: Inside the Clinton White House.* New York: Simon and Schuster, 1994.

Zelikow, Philip, and Condoleezza Rice. *Germany Unified and Europe Transformed: A Study in Statecraft.* Cambridge, Mass.: Harvard University Press, 1995.

ARTICLES

Thanks to the Web, and especially ProQuest, I was able to read many articles from the period. Below are some of those I found most influential.

Apple, R. W., Jr. "Similarities Mark Texas Rivals." *New York Times*, October 30, 1970.

Donovan, Robert. "President Sweeps All Sections of Country Excepting Deep South." *Los Angeles Times*, November 4, 1964.

Dowd, Maureen, and Thomas Friedman. "The Fabulous Bush and Baker Boys." *New York Times Magazine*, May 6, 1990.

Evans, Rowland, and Robert Novak. "The GOP's Southern Star." *Washington Post*, November 1, 1970.

———. "Vice President Bush . . . ?" *Los Angeles Times*, June 5, 1968.

Kasindorf, Martin. "Divining the George Bush Ex-Presidency." *Los Angeles Times*, July 23, 1995.

Rauch, Jonathan. "Father Superior: Our Greatest Modern President." *New Republic*, May 22, 2000.

Roberts, Jerry. "Last Push in New Hampshire." *San Francisco Chronicle*, February 16, 1988.

Reed, Roy. "George Bush on the Move." *New York Times Magazine*, February 10, 1980.

Wead, Doug. "George Bush: Where Does He Stand?" *Christian Herald*, June 1986.

Woodward, Bob. "Making Choices: Bush's Economic Record." *Washington Post*, October 4, 1992; October 5, 1992; October 6, 1992; October 7, 1992.

ARCHIVAL SOURCES AND GOVERNMENT REPORTS

George Bush Presidential Library and Museum, College Station, Texas. Bush Vice Presidential Records (Office of the Chief of Staff, Craig Fuller Subject Files, AIDS).

China Diary.

FOIA Case Numbers 1999-0727-F (Hurricane Andrew), 1999-0277-F (Chief of Staff Samuel K. Skinner), 1998-0206F (David Souter), 1999-0137-F (Vice President Bush's Task Force on Combating Terrorism).

United Nations Diary.

Lyndon B. Johnson Presidential Library and Museum, Austin, Texas.

Central Files, Executive, HU2, box 6; Central Files, box 53, LE/Fl 11-4; "George Bush," Post-Presidential Name File, box 22.

Richard Nixon Library and Birthplace (now Richard Nixon Presidential Library and Museum), Yorba Linda, California.

"George Bush" file.

Nixon Presidential Materials Project (now Richard Nixon Presidential Library and Museum), College Park, Maryland.

Haldeman, box 168, Alpha Subject Files.

Rockefeller Archive Center, Sleepy Hollow, New York.

Interviews with Nelson Rockefeller, October 4, 1977; November 22, 1977.

Tower, John. *The Report of the President's Special Review Board* [Tower Commission Report]. New York: Bantam, February 1987.

Walsh, Lawrence E. *Final Report of Independent Counsel for Iran-Contra Matters* (August 4, 1993). http://www.fas.org., accessed July 1, 2007.

Acknowledgments

"Are you sure you want to do Bush?" Arthur Schlesinger asked me in 2002. Although we were on the telephone, I could sense a mischievous twinkle in his eye. For more than a decade Arthur had generously given of his time to tutor me on John F. Kennedy. True to form, when I said "yes" he generously endorsed my working on a Republican president. Arthur died before reading—and no doubt greatly improving—this book. Fortunately, his historical work will live forever, but I will miss laughing over martinis with him.

A few people stand out in helping to clarify my thinking about George H. W. Bush. Jonathan Rauch, the first great Bush revisionist, shared his brilliant articles with me and discussed the forty-first president; Doug Brinkley generously guided me through the Reagan diaries; Jacob Weisberg and David Greenberg supplied superb ideas; and last, but not least, I am indebted to my former colleague at the University of Virginia's Miller Center of Public Affairs James Sterling Young, who supervised the George Bush Presidential Oral History Project.

Books are impossible (and not much fun to do) without friends. Marilyn Young and Gloria Naftali each helped to make a summer spent writing in Greenwich Village possible and great fun. My teacher Fred Holborn shared a lifetime of thinking about presidents and his political stories, and kindly left me (and Landon Thomas) his magnificent library. Thanks also to Zach Karabell, Bart Aronson, David Coleman, Robert Feldman, Adam Freedman, Shane Harris, Elaine Hatfield, Neil Hultgren, Kent Germany, Steve Knott, Rob Long, Ken Pollack, Dick Rapson, Gideon Rose, Dan Staley, Brewer S. Stone, Matt Waxman, and Fareed Zakaria, who all love politics and yet manage not to take life too seriously.

Paul Golob, my editor at Times Books, was indispensable in making this book worth reading. And as this manuscript neared publication, Sean Wilentz provided a set of superb suggestions when he gracefully stepped in to carry Arthur's project forward. Lauren Fend, Shaun Hong, and my dear friend Laura Moranchek Hussain each supplied critical research materials. Regina Greenwall at the Lyndon Baines Johnson Presidential Library and Museum, the archivists at the George Bush Presidential Library and Museum, Amy Fitch at the Rockefeller Archive Center, Greg Cumming (then) at the private Richard Nixon Library and Birthplace, and Sam Rushay at the Nixon Presidential Materials Project all patiently helped me find my way through materials relating to George H. W. Bush. And John Hawkins, my agent, did his very best—with a smile and a sympathetic shrug—to help me manage the many writing projects I wanted to do simultaneously.

I was not yet done with this project when I got into the presidential library business myself. I'd like to thank Archivist of the United States Allen Weinstein, Assistant Archivist Sharon Fawcett, and the executive director of the Richard Nixon Library and Birthplace Foundation, the Reverend John H. Taylor, for giving me a chance to help make the new federal Richard Nixon Presidential Library and Museum a nonpartisan, transparent, and accessible institution. Meanwhile, my special assistant, Paul Musgrave, deserves equally special mention both for working valiantly to preserve some of my evenings and weekends, so that I could finish this book, and for always making me smarter.

As ever, my family was a source of good cheer and support. My mother, Marge Naftali; my sister, Debbie; and brother-in-law, Serge Lacroix were a great help. Zoe and her brother, A. J. Lacroix, and my other godson, Brewer Dylan Stone, are bubbly reminders that history has a future.

Index

ABOUT THE AUTHOR

TIMOTHY NAFTALI is the director of the Richard Nixon Presidential Library and Museum, having previously served as director of the Presidential Recordings Program at the University of Virginia. A frequent contributor to Slate and NPR, he is the coauthor of the award-winning *Khrushchev's Cold War: The Inside Story of an American Adversary* and of *One Hell of a Gamble: Khrushchev, Castro, and Kennedy, 1958–1964*, and the author of *Blind Spot: The Secret History of American Counterterrorism*. He lives in Los Angeles.